Sir Alan Herbert was born in 1890 and educated at Winchester and Oxford. Having achieved a first in Jurisprudence, he then joined the Royal Navy and served both at Gallipoli and in France during the First World War. He was called to the Bar in 1918, and went on to become a Member of Parliament for Oxford University from 1935 to 1950.

Throughout his life A P Herbert was a prolific writer, delighting his many readers with his witty observations and social satires in the columns of *Punch*. He was the creator of a host of colourful characters – notably Topsy, Albert Haddock and Mr Honeybubble – and wrote novels, poems, musicals, essays, sketches and articles. He was also a tireless campaigner for reform, a denouncer of injustice and a dedicated conserver of the Thames.

By the time of his death in 1971, he had gained a considerable following and was highly regarded in literary circles. J M Barrie, Hilaire Belloc, Rudyard Kipling and John Galsworthy all delighted in his work, and H G Wells applauded him saying, 'You are the greatest of great men. You can raise delightful laughter and that is the only sort of writing that has real power over people like me.'

Light Articles Only

A P Herbert

Illustrated by Geo. Morrow

HOUSE OF
STRATUS

This edition published in 2001 by House of Stratus, an imprint of
Stratus Holdings plc, 24c Old Burlington Street, London, W1X 1RL, UK.
Also at: Suite 210, 1270 Avenue of the Americas, New York, NY 10020, USA.

www.houseofstratus.com

Typeset, printed and bound by House of Stratus.

A catalogue record for this book is available from the British Library
and the Library of Congress.

ISBN 1-84232-588-4

DEDICATED WITH RESPECT TO
LESLIE SCOTT, KC, MP

CONTENTS

Most of these pieces have appeared in the pages of *Punch*, and I have to thank the Proprietors of that paper for their courtesy in permitting me to republish. "The Book of Jonah" appeared in *The London Mercury*, "The Supreme Court" in *The Outlook*, "The Art of Drawing" and "Reading Without Tears" in *Land and Water*, which perished a few weeks later. I thank them all.

A P H

WRONG NUMBERS

I have invented a new telephone game. It is a thoroughly discreditable, anti-social game, and I am not proud of it, but it has been forced upon me by circumstances. It is now clear that my telephone number is the only one the operators know, and my game follows the lines of all the best modern movements, the principle of which is that, if you cannot hit the man you are annoyed with, you hit somebody else instead. Nowadays, when some perfect stranger is introduced to me in error on the telephone, I no longer murmur, "Wrong number, I'm afraid," in my usual accents of sweet sympathy, cool resignation, irritation, hatred or black despair; I pretend that it is the right number. I lead my fellow-victim on into a morass of mystification; I worm out his precious secrets; I waste his precious time. If you can square your conscience you will find it is a glorious game, though I ought to add that considerable skill is required. It is best, perhaps, to make a general rule of answering the call in the first instance in a high feminine voice, as much like a housemaid, or a charwoman, or a Government typist as possible; then you are prepared for any development.

The following are some of the best matches I have played:

I

Me. Hullo!
A Voice. Is that the Midland Railway?
Me. Yes, Madam. Which department do you require?

1

"A Glorious Game."

A V. It's about some eggs. An egg box was despatched from Hitchin –

Me (*obsequious*). I will put you through to the Goods and Transit Department, Madam.

A V (*fervent*). Oh, *thank you!*

Me (*after a short stroll round the garden – in a gruff railway-voice*). Hullo! Motor-vans and Haulage Department –

A V. Oh, it's about some *eggs*. An egg box –

Me (*more in sorrow than in anger*). You require the Goods and Transit Department. I will put you through.

A V. Oh, *thank* you!

Me (*after planting a few more of those confounded cuttings – very suddenly*). The 4.45 to Bunby Major is suspended, Sir.

A V (*apologetic*). I want to speak about some eggs –

Me (*horrified*). Some *legs!*

A V (*patient*). No, some *eggs*: – E – double G – S, eggs. An egg box was despatched from Hitchin by a friend of mine on the 21st –

Me (*sharply*). What name, Madam?

A V. Major Bludyer. It was despatched on –

Me. Is he one of the Buckinghamshire Bludyers?

A V. What? Hullo!… Hullo! It was despatched on –

Me. I mean, is he *the* Major Bludyer – that well-grown old boy? From what I know of his eggs –

A V (*growing fainter*). I can't hear you very well. It's about some *eggs* –

Me. Well, I'm very glad to have had this little talk. Remember me to old Bludyer. Goodbye.

II

Me (*squeaky*). Hullo!

A Voice (*businesslike, in a great hurry*). Hullo! Is that you, Mortimer?

Me (*very deliberate*). Mr Mortimer is in the next room. If you will hold the line I will fetch him. Who is it speaking, please?

A V. Oh, never mind that.

Me (firm). Who is it speaking, please?

A V. Oh, da—! Say it's George. And be quick, please.

Me (after a good deal of unavoidable delay). Hullo, George!

A V. Hullo, Mortimer! You *have* been a time! Look here – about this meeting: have you got your minutes ready yet?

Me. Not quite. Practically. I was just doing them –

A V. Oh! Well, it's like this: I've had a talk with Sir Donald and he thinks you'd better leave out that scene about Atkins and the Debentures. He thinks we might have trouble with the Manchester lot if you read that out, but if you don't say anything about it they'll never know –

Me. You dirty dog!

A V. What's that?

Me (innocent). I didn't say anything. I think there's someone on the line – (*in a brand-new voice*) Cuckoo!

A V (indignant). I say, Sir, do you mind getting off the line? Hullo! Hullo!… He's gone now. Well, don't forget that. So long, old man. Sorry you couldn't come round the other night; I wanted you to meet my *fiancée* – you haven't, have you?

Me. Which one?

A V (skittishly). You old ass – Miss Tickle, of course.

Me. Oh, I know *her.* As a matter of fact I was engaged to her myself once – but that's many years ago.

A V. What's that? You sound as if you'd got a cold.

Me. I rather think I have. You always make such a draught down the telephone. Goodbye, old man.

III

A Voice. Is that the Box Office?

Me. Which Box Office?

A V. Is that the Paragon Theatre?

Me. Yes, Madam.

A V. Oh, have you two seats for next Thursday?

Me. Yes, Madam. There is a stall in row D, and I have one seat left in the back row of the dress circle – a very good view of the stage, Madam.

A V. Oh, but I want them *together*.

Me. I'm afraid we never sell seats *together*, Madam. The Lord Chamberlain –

A V. Oh, but –

Me. May I ask why you want to see this play, Madam?

A V. I can't hear you… Hullo!

Me. I mean, between ourselves, it's a thoroughly bad adaptation of a thoroughly bad foreign play thoroughly badly acted by a rotten lot of actors. *Letty Loo* is perfectly awful, and there's no room for your legs, unless you would care for a box, and there isn't one if you would; so if I were you I should stay quietly at home with Henry. *Au revoir!*

IV

A Voice (*most important*). Hullo! Is that the Treasury?

Me (*sweetly feminine*). Treasury speaking.

A V (*as if the end of the world was in sight*). I want to speak to the Prime Minister's Private Secretary.

Me. The Prime Minister's Private Secretary is engaged. I can put you through to the Whips' Office.

A V (*angrily*). I don't *want* the Whips' Office, I want –

Me. One moment, please.

[*A good many moments pass.*]

A V (*menacing*). Hullo! Hullo! Hullo!

Me (*sweetly, as if conferring some priceless boon*). Put *three* pennies in the slot and *turn* the handle, please.

A V (*spluttering*). Look here, put me through to the supervisor at once.

Me (*very far off*). Supervisor speaking.

A V (*with suppressed passion, yet pompous withal*). Look here – I'm a Member of Parliament. I've been –

Me (*gently*). Do not shout into the receiver, please.

5

A V. Hullo! I'm a –

Me. Do not say "Hullo!"

A V (*maddened*). What's that? Hullo! Look here – I'm a Member of Parliament, and I've been trying for *half an hour* to get through to the Prime Minister's –

Me. I am sorry you have been trrrr-roubled. You are *thrrrrough* now.

A V. Hullo! Is that the Prime Minister's Private Secretary?

Me (*quiet, weary and competent*). Which one do you want?

A V. Hullo! Sir Thingummy Jig speaking. I want to speak to the Prime Minister's –

Me. Yes, I heard that. But do you want the Principal Private Secretary, or the Assistant Principal Private Secretary, or one of the Personal Private Secretaries? I mean there are forty-seven of us altogether and it makes a lot of difference –

A V (*weakening*). I can't quite hear. Perhaps you can help me. It's about –

Me. One moment, please. Here is the Prime Minister himself. Would you mind speaking to *him*? I'm rather busy.

A V (*awestruck*). Of course… Hullo!

Me. Hullo!… The Prime Minister speaking… Look here, Jig, I want to have a word with you. Would you mind holding the line a moment while I speak to my secretary?

A V (*fawning*). By all means… There's no hurry – no hurry at all.

As far as I know the poor fellow is holding still.

THE GENIUS OF MR BRADSHAW

No one will be surprised to hear that the Christian name of Mr Bradshaw was George. Indeed, it is difficult to think what other name a man of his calibre could have had. But many people will be surprised to hear that Mr Bradshaw is no longer alive. Whatever one thinks of his work one is inclined to think of him as a living personality, working laboriously at some terminus – probably at the Charing Cross Hotel. But it is not so. He died, in fact, in 1853. His first book – or rather the first edition of his book[*] – was published in 1839; yet, unlike the author, it still lives. He is, in fact, the supreme example of the posthumous serial writer. I have no information about Mr Debrett and Mr Burke, but the style and substance of their work are relatively so flimsy that one is justified, I think, in neglecting them. In any case their public is a limited one. So, of course, is Mr Bradshaw's; but it is better than theirs. Mr Debrett's book we read idly in an idle hour; when we read Mr Bradshaw's it is because we feel that we simply must; and that perhaps is the surest test of genius.

It is no wonder that in some circles Mr Bradshaw holds a position comparable only to the position of Homer. I once knew an elderly clergyman who knew the whole of Mr Bradshaw's book by heart. He could tell you without hesitation the time of any train from anywhere to anywhere else. He looked forward

* "Bradshaw's General Railway and Steam Navigation Guide for Great Britain and Ireland."

each month to the new number as other people look forward to the new numbers of magazines. When it came he skimmed eagerly through its pages and noted with a fierce excitement that they had taken off the 5.30 from Larne Harbour, or that the 7.30 from Galashiels was stopping that month at Shankend. He knew all the connections; he knew all the restaurant trains; and, if you mentioned the 6.15 to Little Buxton, he could tell you offhand whether it was a Saturdays Only or a Saturdays Excepted.

This is the exact truth, and I gathered that he was not unique. It seems that there is a Bradshaw cult; there may even be a Bradshaw club, where they meet at intervals for Bradshaw dinners, after which a paper is read on "Changes I have made, with some Observations on Salisbury." I suppose some of them have first editions, and talk about them very proudly; and they have hot academic discussions on the best way to get from Barnham Junction to Cardiff without going through Bristol. Then they drink the toast of "The Master" and go home in omnibuses. My friend was a schoolmaster and took a small class of boys in Bradshaw; he said they knew as much about it as he did. I call that corrupting the young.

But apart from this little band of admirers I am afraid that the book does suffer from neglect. Who is there, for example, who has read the "Directions" on page 1, where we are actually shown the method of reading tentatively suggested by the author himself? The ordinary reader, coming across a certain kind of thin line, lightly dismisses it as a misprint or a restaurant car on Fridays. If he had read the Preface he would know that it meant a SHUNT. He would know that a SHUNT means that passengers are enabled to continue their journey by changing into the next train. Whether he would know what that means I do not know. The best authorities suppose it to be a poetical way of saying that you have to change – what is called an euphemism.

"If he had read the Preface he would know that it meant a
SHUNT."

No, you must not neglect the Preface; and you must not neglect the Appendix on Hotels. As sometimes happens in works of a philanthropic character, Mr Bradshaw's Appendix has a human charm that is lacking in his treatment of his principal theme, the arrival and departure of trains. To the careful student it reveals also a high degree of organization among his collaborators, the hotel managers. It is obvious, for example, that at Bournemouth there must be at least one hotel which has the finest situation on the south coast. Indeed one would expect to find that there was more than one. But no; Bournemouth, exceptionally fortunate in having at once the most select hotel on the south coast, the largest and best-appointed hotel on the south coast and the largest and most up-to-date hotel on the south coast, has positively only one which has the finest position on the south coast. Indeed, there is only one of these in the whole of England, though there are two which have the finest position on the east coast.

How is it, we wonder, that with so much variation on a single theme such artistic restraint is achieved? It is clear, I think, that before they send in their manuscripts the hotel managers must meet somewhere and agree together the exact terms of their contributions to the book. "The George" agrees that for the coming year "The Crown" shall have the "finest cuisine in England," provided "The George" may have "the most charming situation imaginable," and so on. I should like to be at one of those meetings.

This is the only theory which accounts for the curious phrases we find so frequently in the text: "*Acknowledged* to be the finest"; "*Admittedly* in the best position." Who is it that acknowledges or admits these things? It must be the other managers at these annual meetings. Yes, the restraint of the collaborators is wonderful, and in one point only has it broken down. There are no fewer than seventeen hotels with an Unrivalled Situation, and two of these are at Harrogate. For a small place like the British Isles it seems to me that this is too many.

For the rest, what imagery, what exaltation we find in this Appendix! Dazed with imagined beauty we pass from one splendid haunt to another. One of them has *three* golf courses of its own; several are *replete* with every comfort (and is not "replete" the perfect epithet?). Here is a seductive one "on the sea edge," and another whose principal glory is its sanitary certificate. Another stands on the spot where Tennyson received his inspiration for the *Idylls of the King*, and leaves it at that. In such a spot even "cuisine" is negligible.

On the whole, from a literary point of view, the hydros come out better than the mere hotels. But of course they have unequalled advantages. With such material as Dowsing Radiant Heat, D'Arsonval High Frequency and Fango Mud Treatment almost any writer could be sensational. What is High Frequency, I wonder? It is clear, at any rate, that it would be madness to have a hydro without it.

Well, I have selected my hotel – on purely literary grounds. Or rather I have selected two. One is the place where they have the Famous Whirlpool Baths. I shall go there at once.

The manager of the other is a great artist; alone among the collaborators he understands simplicity. His contribution occupies a whole page; but there is practically nothing in it, nothing about cuisine or sanitation, or elegance, or comfort. Only, in the middle, he writes, quite simply:

THE MOST PERFECT HOTEL IN THE WORLD.

FIVE INCHES

THE GREAT JOKE

They came and split a turkey with us on Boxing Day, ten old soldiers, all out of a job, and only ten legs between them. At least there were only ten real legs; two of them had admirable imitation ones, and there were sixteen excellent crutches. One of them was a miner – *was*, of course; just now he is not mining much; perhaps that is why he seemed such a decent fellow, not at all violent or unpleasant, as one knows those practising miners are. In fact he reminded one of the miners one used to have in one's platoon. Personally I had the honour to have a whole platoon of them. Odd, isn't it, what capital fellows they were then, and how sadly they deteriorate when they get back to the mines? And it was odd, too, to hear this fellow say that he wished he could be back in the pits; I thought it was such a hateful and dangerous occupation.

Yes, he was a nice miner, and so were the rest of them, very cheerful and respectful. But they didn't talk much – at first. It was strangely difficult to find a safe subject. A few years ago there would have been no difficulty; one would have talked war-shop. "Were you ever at Ypres?" "I was on Gallipoli." "Did you know Captain — ?" and so on. We did a little of this, but it didn't go really well.

In the dining room I keep a large coloured photograph of the top of the Vimy Ridge on the day of a battle – you know the sort of thing, a hideous expanse of broken brown earth, that dreadful endless brown, with walls of smoke all round the horizon, shells bursting in the middle distance, a battered trench in the foreground, with a few scattered men climbing out of it, gazing at the camera with expressionless faces, stretcher-bearers stooping on the parapet with their stretchers on their shoulders, odd men straying everywhere like lost sheep across the chocolate wilderness, looking aimless, looking small.

Our guests were interested in that picture; it was wonderfully *like*, they said; but I felt that my usual remark about it was hardly suitable. Usually I tell my guests, and it is true, that I keep the picture as a kind of chastener, so that, when I am moved to complain at the troubles of this world, I can look at the picture and think, "At any rate life is better than it was then – " It was on the tip of my tongue to say so to the one-legged men when it came to me that for them, perhaps, at the moment, it wasn't true.

After the turkey and the pudding and the crackers, and of course the beer, there was a slight thaw, but it was still very difficult. We tried to get them to sing. Only a few years ago how easy it was. There was "Tipperary" and many another rousing chorus. One was familiar in those times with the popular songs of the day. Unfortunately these were the only songs we could produce now. And they didn't suit. "Keep the Home Fires Burning," for instance – one didn't like to suggest that. The chief minstrel of the one-legged men, who was also the chief comedian, disinterred from a heap of old music, "Your King and Country Need You." "How would that go, Bert?" he said. He said it without bitterness, I don't know why, and Bert's answer was a silent grin, and one felt that Bert was right. "Pack up your Troubles in your old Kit-bag," "Till the Boys Come Home" – all the old titles had a certain ironic underlining in that company.

So we abandoned singing and we sat rather silent. There was some desultory conversation about the various "trades" to which a grateful State had trained them, and left it at that; there was some mild chaff of Bill, who had been too old (at thirty-five) to be trained at all, though not too old to learn musketry and lose a leg; but socially one felt the "party" was drifting to disaster.

It was saved, like many parties, by "shop," and not war-shop, at least not exactly. What sort of shop will amuse ten one-legged men? Why, one-legged shop, of course. Somebody said, "Is your leg comfortable?" and that set the ball rolling. All the tongues wagged gleefully at once; all the technical details of one-leggedness, all the points of the various kinds of "legs," were brought out and tossed about and hotly contested as if we had been a number of golfers arguing the merits of different makes of putters. Some of us wear "stump socks"; some of us can't stand the things. Some of us have "buckets" (graphically described) which we can comfortably pad, and some of us have something else not nearly so good. Some of us are excited about the new "alumium" legs, four pounds lighter, which are soon to be available, though we think it a terrible waste of money now that we have most of us got wooden ones. Here is a chance for the "economising" campaigners! Now then, Lord Rothermere, "No Aluminium Legs!" What a war cry! Altogether it is an enthralling topic; there is no more awkwardness…

And it is so amusing. Gad, how we laughed! There was the story of the man on the Underground, a friend of ours. Someone trod on his false foot in the crowded train and, scrambling out in a hurry at a station, he found himself footless on the platform, while the train slid away with the other fellow still standing on his foot. Ha, ha! how we laughed.

But most of us are "above-the-knee," and that provides the best joke of all. You see it all depends on the length of your stump (or "stoomp"). If you have five inches left you get an eighty per cent pension; if you have more you get less – even if it is only five and a quarter. That quarter of an inch makes all the difference, financially, though practically it isn't a great deal of use. How much have *you* got? Ah, you're unlucky. I'm four and three-quarters – a near thing, eh? Peals of laughter. "You go back and have another inch off. Ho, ho, ho!" We roll about in our chairs.

Well, well, it's a queer world; but the party was a great success after all.

READING WITHOUT TEARS

I am teaching my daughter to read. It is very difficult. I cannot imagine how I learned to read myself. And when I look at the classic called *Reading Without Tears*, which was, I understand, the foundation of my learning, I am yet more puzzled. The author of the book seems to believe strongly in original sin. In the Preface I read: "Tears must be shed by sinful little creatures subject to waywardness and deserving so many reproofs and corrections"; but reading need not be such an occasion; and again, "Observe their minutest actions; shut not your eyes to their sinful nature; nor believe them *incapable* of injustice or unkindness, of deceit or covetousness." Perhaps this attitude explains the book.

The author's great idea is *pictures*. A is like a hut with a window upstairs. B, on the other hand, is like a house with two windows; and little b is like a child with a wide frock coming to you. When I look at the pictures opposite I see what the author means, but when I look at A and B and little b dispassionately by themselves they suggest nothing at all to me. I simply cannot imagine the hut or the house or the child with the wide frock.

But let us look at some more. D is like an old man leaning on a stick; E is like a carriage with a little seat for the driver; G is like a monkey eating a cake. These are no better. Try as I may, I cannot see the little seat for the driver; or, if I do, I see it just as

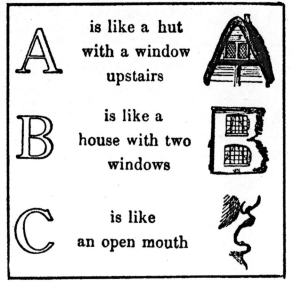

A is like a hut with a window upstairs

B is like a house with two windows

C is like an open mouth

"Did we really…?"

vividly in F. But F is like a tree with a seat for a child. So I know that I am wrong.

Now the pictorial memory is a valuable thing; and this pictorial method of teaching is no doubt valuable.

But surely the pictures are of no real use unless there is some inevitable connection, however slight, between the form of the thing which it is desired to impress on the memory and the picture with which it is compared. My daughter's imagination is, of course, much more vivid than mine, but, even so, I cannot imagine her looking coolly at the naked D and saying, "Yes, that is the old man leaning on a stick." She is more likely to say, "That is the ground floor of the house with two windows," for she has a logical mind. And even if she does not remember the futile picture of the old man in a long shirt with his body bent at right angles to his legs, I don't see why, even then, she should connect him with D. There is nothing peculiarly D-ish about an old man. Yet it seems that I learned my alphabet in this way. I was a clever child, though sinful, I fear.

Then we get on to words. The book follows the first principle of all teachers of languages in arranging that among the first words which the child learns there are as many words as possible which he will never use as a child, and, indeed, will probably never encounter in his entire career. Prominent among the first words in this book are such favourites as *pap*, *bin*, *hob*, *sob*, and *sop*, *emmet* and *tome*. Each of these is printed three times, in a column, like this:

Pat	Pan	Pap
PAT	PAN	PAP
pat	pan	pap

Over each column is a little picture. When you are teaching the child *pap* you say to her: "P-a-P, pap – do you see the pretty picture? That is a nanny with a baby in her lap. She is giving the baby a bottle. The bottle has pap in it. At least, it is not pap, really, but it is called pap for the purposes of the alphabet. You remember the letters, don't you? First there is a big P – *you* know, like a man with a pack on his back. Then a little a, which is like a goose on the water. Then a little p; that is like another man coming to you with a pack on his back. Now we have it all in big letters. Maggie read them out."

Maggie (*firmly*). K.

You. No, no, not K. Don't you remember the picture?

Maggie. Yes, it was a nanny with a baby.

You. No, not that one. It was a man with a pack on his back – P.

Maggie. P.

You. That's right. What comes next?

Maggie. A goose on the water.

You. No, that was the *little* a. This is a big letter. Don't you remember the dear little hut with the window upstairs? What letter was that?

Maggie. B.

You. No, no, that was a *house*, not a *hut*, and it had *two* windows. Don't be so inaccurate. This is a big A. Now, what's next?

Maggie. A little house with a nanny inside. And there's a goose in the garden. And a baby.

You (*patiently*). No, this is another P. He is like a man with a pack on his back. P-A-P pap – there you are. That's very good.

Maggie. May I go into the garden now?

You. Yes.

After that we learn sentences, and we raise in the child's mind a few more simple pictures of Nature by repeating several times such statements as:

A pig had a fig.

The author introduces us to Ben, who can *sup* sop. Ben, however, has a fat pup, and this pup cannot *sip* sop. My daughter, as I said, has a logical mind, and she immediately asked if Ben's pup could *sup* sop. She had perceived at once that if he could neither sip nor sup the unfortunate animal was cut off from sop altogether. I said I didn't know. I don't. But I see that Ben fed Poll on bun, so I expect he gave the pup some too.

It is a pity that the author could not provide pictures for some of the more striking incidents she records. Some of these would do:

I met a cat in a bog
I sat in the bog

A hog is in a bog
A wig is in a bog
A pen is in a bog
I had a red bed
Ten men had a pen
I had a wet hen
I fed ten men in a den

I should have thought that by appropriate illustrations the child might have been helped to a greater knowledge, not only of letters, but of life.

But perhaps the most vivid of all these pages is page 99, which I reproduce verbatim:

A bun is in a tun
A gun is in a tun
A dog is in a tun
A hog is in a tun
A pig is in a tun
A wig is in a tun
A hen is in a tun
A pen is in a tun

NOTE – Let the child begin the book again, if it likes.

What *is* a tun? Until I started out to educate my daughter I did not know. But then, I am not a sinful child. For hush! it seems to be a sort of *barrel*. I have drawn rather a jolly tun myself.

If we could only look back into our childish minds and really recapture the impressions of life (if any) which inhabited us at the end of a day when we had triumphantly mastered page 99 and similar pages, and if one could set those impressions down in print, what rich romances might be born into the world!

But is there no Society for the Protection of Children from This Sort of Book?

"A pen is in a tun."

ON WITH THE DANCE

I have been to a dance; or rather I have been to a fashionable restaurant where dancing is done. I was not invited to a dance – there are very good reasons for that; I was invited to dinner. But many of my fellow-guests have invested a lot of money in dancing. That is to say, they keep on paying dancing instructors to teach them new tricks; and the dancing instructors, who know their business, keep on inventing new tricks. As soon as they have taught everybody a new step they say it is unfashionable and invent a new one. This is all very well, but it means that, in order to keep up with them and get your money's worth out of the last trick you learned, it is necessary during its brief life of respectability to dance at every available opportunity. You dance as many nights a week as is physically possible; you dance on weekdays and you dance on Sundays; you begin dancing in the afternoon and you dance during tea in the coffee rooms of expensive restaurants, whirling your precarious way through littered and abandoned tea tables; and at dinner time you leap up madly before the fish and dance like variety artistes in a highly polished arena before a crowd of complete strangers eating their food; or, as if seized with an uncontrollable craving for the dance, you fling out after the joint for one wild gallop in an outer room, from which you return, perspiring and dyspeptic, to the consumption of an ice-pudding, before dashing forth to the final orgy at a picture

"Faded away."

gallery, where the walls are appropriately covered with pictures of barbaric women dressed for the hot weather.

That is what happened at this dinner. As soon as you had started a nice conversation with a lady a sort of roaring was heard without; her eyes gleamed, her nostrils quivered like those of a horse planning a gallop, and in the middle of one of your best sentences she simply faded away with some horrible man at the other end of the table who was probably "the only man in London who can do the Double Straddle properly." This went on the whole of the meal, and it made connected conversation quite difficult. For my own part I went on eating, and when I had properly digested I went out and looked at the little victims getting their money's worth.

From the door of the room where the dancing was done a confused uproar overflowed, as if several men of powerful physique were banging a number of pokers against a number of saucepans, and blowing whistles, and occasional catcalls, and now and then beating a drum and several sets of huge cymbals, and ceaselessly twanging at innumerable banjos, and at the same time singing in a foreign language, and shouting curses or exhortations or street cries, or imitating hunting calls and the cry of the hyena, or uniting suddenly in the war-whoop of some pitiless Sudan tribe.

It was a really terrible noise. It hit you like the back-blast of an explosion as you entered the room. There was no distinguishable tune. It was simply an enormous noise. But there was a kind of savage rhythm about it which made one think immediately of Indians and fierce men and the native camps one used to visit at the Earl's Court Exhibition. And this was not surprising. For the musicians included one genuine negro and three men with their faces blacked; and the noise and the rhythm were the authentic music of a negro village in South America, and the words which some genius had once set to the noise were an exhortation to go to the place where the negroes dwelt.

To judge by their movements, many of the dancers had, in fact, been there, and had carefully studied the best indigenous models. They were doing some quite extraordinary things. No two couples were doing quite the same thing for more than a few seconds, so that there was an endless variety of extraordinary postures. Some of them shuffled secretly along the edges of the room, their faces tense, their shoulders swaying like reeds in a light wind, their progress almost imperceptible; they did not rotate, they did not speak, but sometimes the tremor of a skirt or the slight stirring of a patent-leather shoe showed that they were indeed alive and in motion, though that motion was as the motion of a glacier, not to be measured in minutes or yards.

And some in a kind of fever rushed hither and thither among the thick crowd, avoiding disaster with marvellous dexterity; and sometimes they revolved slowly and sometimes quickly and sometimes spun giddily round for a moment like gyroscopic tops. Then they too would be seized with a kind of trance, or it may be with sheer shortness of breath, and hung motionless for a little in the centre of the room, while the mad throng jostled and flowed about them like the leaves in autumn round a dead bird.

And some did not revolve at all, but charged straightly up and down; and some of these thrust their loves for ever before them, as the Prussians thrust the villagers in the face of the enemy, and some for ever navigated themselves backwards like moving breakwaters to protect their darlings from the rude, precipitate seas.

Some of them kept themselves as upright as possible, swaying slightly like willows from the hips, and some of them contorted themselves into strange and angular shapes, now leaning perilously forward till they were practically lying upon their terrified partners, and now bending sideways as a man bends who has water in one ear after bathing. All of them clutched each other in a close and intimate manner, but some, as if by separation to intensify the joy of their union, or perhaps to secure greater freedom for some particularly spacious manoeuvre, would part suddenly in the middle of the room and, clinging distantly with their hands, execute a number of complicated side-steps in opposite directions, or aim a series of vicious kicks at each other, after which they would reunite in a passionate embrace and gallop in a frenzy round the room, or fall into a trance, or simply fall down. If they fell down they lay still for a moment in the fearful expectation of death, as men lie who fall under a horse; and then they would creep on hands and knees to the wall through the whirling and indifferent crowd.

Watching them, you could not tell what any one couple would do next. The most placid and dignified among them might at any moment fling a leg out behind them and almost kneel in mutual adoration, and then, as if nothing unusual had happened, shuffle onward through the press; or, as though some electric mechanism had been set in motion, they would suddenly lift a foot sideways and stand on one leg. Poised pathetically, as if waiting for the happy signal when they might put the other leg down, these men looked very sad, and I wished that the Medusa's head might be smuggled somehow into the room for their attitudes to be imperishably recorded in cold stone; it would have been a valuable addition to modern sculpture.

Upon this whirlpool I embarked with the greatest misgiving and a strange young woman clinging to my person. The noise was deafening. The four black men were now all shouting at once and playing all their instruments at once, working up to the inconceivable uproar of the finale; and all the dancers began to dance with a last desperate fury. Bodies buffeted one from behind, and while one was yet looking round in apology or anger more bodies buffeted one from the flank. It was like swimming in a choppy sea, where there is no time to get the last wave out of your mouth before the next one hits you.

Close beside us a couple fell down with a great crash. I looked at them with concern, but no one else took any notice. On with the dance! Faster and faster the black men played. I was dimly aware now that they were standing on their chairs, bellowing, and fancied the end must be near. Then we were washed into a quiet backwater, in a corner, and from here I determined never to issue till the Last Banjo should indeed sound. Here I sidled vaguely about for a long time, hoping that I looked like a man preparing for some vast culminating feat, a side-step or a buzz or a double-Jazz-spin or an ordinary fall down.

The noise suddenly ceased; the four black men had exploded.

"Very good exercise," my partner said.

"Quite," said I.

THE AUTOBIOGRAPHY

John Antony Grunch was one of the mildest, most innocent men I ever knew. He had a wife to whom he was devoted with a dog-like devotion; he went to church; he was shy and reserved, and he held a mediocre position in a firm of envelope-makers in the City. But he had a romantic soul, and whenever the public craving for envelopes fell off – and that is seldom – he used to allay his secret passion for danger, devilry and excitement by writing sensational novels. One of these was recently published, and John Antony is now dead. The novel did it.

Yet it was a very mild sort of "shocker," about a very ordinary murder. The villain simply slew one of his typists in the counting house with a sword-umbrella and concealed his guilt by putting her in a pillar box. But it had "power," and it was very favourably reviewed. One critic said that "the author, who was obviously a woman, had treated with singular delicacy and feeling the ever-urgent problem of female employment in our great industrial centres." Another said that the book was "a brilliant burlesque of the fashionable type of detective fiction." Another wrote that "it was a conscientious analysis of a perplexing phase of agricultural life." John thought that must refer to the page where he had described the allotments at Shepherd's Bush. But he was pleased and surprised by what they said.

What he did *not* like was the interpretation offered by his family and his friends, who at once decided that the work was the autobiography of John Antony. You see, the scene was laid in London, and John lived in London; the murdered girl was a typist, and there were two typists in John's office; and, to crown all, the villain in the book had a boar hound, and John himself had a Skye terrier. The thing was as plain as could be. Men he met in the City said, "How's that boar hound of yours?" or "I like that bit where you hit the policeman. When did you do that?" "*You*," mark you. Old friends took him aside and whispered, "Very sorry to hear you don't hit it off with Mrs

"Off with that adventuress."

Grunch; I always thought you were such a happy couple." His wife's family said, "Poor Gladys! what a life she must have had!" His own family said, "Poor John! what a life she must have led him to make him go off with that adventuress!" Several people identified the adventuress as Miss Crook, the Secretary of the local Mothers' Welfare League, of which John was a vice-president.

The fog of suspicion swelled and spread and penetrated into every cranny and level of society. No servants would come near the house, or if they did they soon stumbled on a copy of the shocker while doing the drawing room, read it voraciously and rushed screaming out of the front door. When he took a parcel of washing to the post office the officials refused to accept it until he had opened it and shown that there were no bodies in it.

The animal kingdom is very sensitive to the suspicion of guilt. John noticed that dogs avoided him, horses neighed at him, earwigs fled from him in horror, caterpillars madly spun

"Two detectives waiting."

themselves into cocoons as he approached, owls hooted, snakes hissed. Only Mrs Grunch remained faithful.

But one morning at breakfast Mrs Grunch said, "Pass the salt, please, John." John didn't hear. He was reading a letter. Mrs Grunch said again, "Pass the salt, please, John." John was still engrossed. Mrs Grunch wanted the salt pretty badly, so she got up and fetched it. As she did so she noticed that the handwriting of the letter was the handwriting of A Woman. Worse, it was written on the embossed paper of the Mothers' Welfare League. It must be from Miss Crook. *And it was*. It was about the annual outing. "Ah, ha!" said Mrs Grunch. (I am afraid that "Ah, ha!" doesn't really convey to you the sort of sound she made, but you must just imagine.) "Ah, ha! So *that's* why you couldn't pass the salt!"

Mad with rage, hatred, fear, chagrin, pique, jealousy and indigestion, John rushed out of the house and went to the office. At the door of the office he met one of the typists. He held the door open for her. She simpered and refused to go in front of him. Being still mad with rage, hatred, chagrin and all those other things, John made a cross gesture with his umbrella. With a shrill, shuddering shriek of "Murderer!" the girl cantered violently down Ludgate Hill and was never seen again. Entering the office, John found two detectives waiting to ask him a few questions in connection with the Newcastle Pigsty Murder, which had been done with some pointed instrument, probably an umbrella.

After that *The Daily Horror* rang up and asked if he would contribute an article to their series on "Is Bigamy Worthwhile?"

Having had enough rushing for one day John walked slowly out into the street, trying to remember the various ways in which his characters had committed suicide. He threw himself over the Embankment wall into the river, but fell in a dinghy which he had not noticed; he bought some poison, but the chemist recognised his face from a photograph in the Literary Column of *The Druggist* and gave him ipecacuanha (none of you can spell that); he thought of cutting his throat, but broke his thumbnail trying to open the big blade, and gave it up. Desperate, he decided to go home. At Victoria he was hustled along the platform on the pretence that there is more room in the rear of trains. Finally he was hustled on to the line and electrocuted.

And everybody said, "So it *was* true."

THE WHITE SPAT

When it is remembered how large a part has been played in history by revolutionary and political songs it is both lamentable and strange that at the present time only one of the numerous political faiths has a hymn of its own – "The Red Flag." The author of the words owes a good deal, I should say, to the author of "Rule Britannia," though I am inclined to think he has gone one better. The tune is that gentle old tune which we used to know as "Maryland," and by itself it rather suggests a number of tired sheep waiting to go through a gate than a lot of people thinking very redly. I fancy the author realised this, and he has got over it by putting in some good powerful words like "scarlet," "traitors," "flinch" and "dungeon," whenever the tune is particularly sheepish. The effect is effective. Just imagine if the Middle Classes Union could march down the middle of the Strand singing that fine chorus:

> "Then raise the scarlet standard high
> Beneath its shade we'll live and die;
> Though cowards flinch and traitors sneer
> We'll keep the Red Flag flying here."

Well, I have set myself to supply some other parties with songs, and I have begun with "The White Spat," which is to be the party hymn of the High Tories (if any). I have written it to the same tune as "The Red Flag," because, when the lion finally does lie down with the lamb, it will be much more convenient if they can bleat and roar in the same metre, and I shall hope to hear Mr Robert Williams and Lord Robert Cecil singing these two songs at once one day. I am not wholly satisfied with "The White Spat," but I think I have caught the true spirit, or, at any rate, the proper inconsequence of these things:

THE WHITE SPAT

Air – *Maryland*

> The spats we wear are pure as snow –
> We are so careful where we go;
> We don't go near the vulgar bus
> Because it always splashes us.
>
> *Chorus.* We take the road with trustful hearts,
> Avoiding all the messy parts;
> However dirty you may get
> We'll keep the White Spat spotless yet.
>
> At night there shines a special star
> To show us where the puddles are;

The crossing-sweeper sweeps the floor –
That's what the crossing-sweeper's for.
Chorus. Then take the road, etc., etc.

I know it doesn't look much, just written down on paper; but you try singing it and you'll find you're carried away.

Of course there ought to be an international verse, but I'm afraid I can't compete with the one in my model:

"Look round: the Frenchman loves its blaze,
 The sturdy German chants its praise;
 In Moscow's vaults its hymns are sung;
 Chicago swells the surging throng."

This is the best I can do:

"From Russia's snows to Afric's sun
 The race of spatriots is one;
 One faith unites their alien blood –
 There's nothing to be said for mud."

Now we have the song of the Wee Frees. I wanted this to be rather pathetic, but I'm not sure that I haven't overdone it. The symbolism, though, is well-nigh perfect, and, after all, the symbolism is the chief thing. This goes to the tune of "Annie Laurie":

THE OLD BLACK BROLLY

Air – *Annie Laurie*

Under the Old Umbrella,
  Beneath the leaking gamp,
Wrapped up in woolly phrases
  We battle with the damp.
  Come, gather round the gamp!

Observe, it is pre-war;
    And beneath the old Black Brolly
There's room for several more.

Shameless calumniators
    Calumniate like mad;
Detractors keep detracting;
    It really is too bad;
    It really is too bad.
To show we're not quite dead,
    We wave the old Black Brolly
And hit them on the head.

"The National."

Then we have the National Party. I am rather vague about the National Party, but I know they are frightfully military, and they keep on having Mass Rallies in Kensington – complete with drums, I expect. Where all the masses come from I don't quite know, as a prolonged search has failed to reveal anyone who knows anyone who is actually a member of the party. Everybody tells me, though, that there is at least one Brigadier-General (Tempy) mixed up with it, if not two, and at least one Lord, though possibly one of the Brigadiers is the same as the Lord; but after all they represent the Nation, so they ought to have a song. They have nothing but "Rule Britannia" now, I suppose.

Their song goes to the tune of "The British Grenadiers." I have written it as a duet, but no doubt other parts could be added if the occasion should ever arise.*

THE NATIONAL

Air – *The British Grenadiers*

Some talk of Coalitions,
   Of Tories and all that;
They are but cheap editions
   Of the one and only Nat.;
Our Party has no equals,
   Though of course it has its peers,
With a tow, row, row, row, row, row,
   For the British Brigadiers.

You have no idea how difficult it is to write down the right number of *rows* first time; however I daresay the General wouldn't mind a few extra ones.

* I understand that it has not arisen. On the contrary…

We represent the Nation
　　As no one else can do;
Without exaggeration
　　Our membership is two.
We rally in our masses
　　And give three hearty cheers,
With a tow, row, row, row, row, row
　　For the National Brigadiers.

There could be a great deal more of that, but perhaps you have had enough.

Of course, if you don't think the poetry of my songs is good enough, I shall just have to quote some of "The International" words to show you that it's the *tune* that matters.

Here you are:

"Arise! ye starvelings from your slumbers,
　　Arise! ye criminals of want,
For reason in revolt now thunders,
　　And at last ends the age of cant."

If people can grow excited singing that, my songs would send them crazy.

Then there is the Coalition. I have had a good deal of difficulty about this, but I think that at last I have hit the right note; all my first efforts were too dignified. This goes to a darkie tune:

THE PIEBALD MARE

Air – *Camptown Ladies*

Down-town darkies all declare,
　　Doo-dah, doo-dah,

There never was a hoss like the piebald mare
    Doo-dah, doo-dah day!
One half dark and the other half pale,
    Doo-dah, doo-dah,
Two fat heads and a great big tail,
    Doo-dah, doo-dah day!

Chorus. Gwine to run all night,
    Gwine to run all day!
I put my money on the piebald mare
    Because she run both way.

Little old DAVE he ride dat hoss,
    Doo-dah, doo-dah,
Where'll she be if he takes a toss?
    Doo-dah, doo-dah day!
De people try to push him off,
    Doo-dah, doo-dah,
De more dey push de more he scoff,
    Doo-dah, doo-dah day!

Chorus. Gwine to run, etc.

Over the largest fence they bound,
    Doo-dah, doo-dah,
Things exploding all around,
    Doo-dah, doo-dah day!
One fine day dat hoss will burst,
    Doo-dah, doo-dah,
But little old DAVE he'll *walk* in first,
    Doo-dah, doo-dah day!

Chorus. Gwine to run, etc.

Once again, merely written down, the words do *not* thrill, but I hope none of the parties will definitely reject these hymns till they have heard them actually sung; if necessary I will give a trial rendering myself.

The other day, when we were playing charades and had to act L, we did *Lloyd George and the Coalition*; and the people who were acting the Coalition sang the above song with really wonderful effect. It is true that the other side thought we were acting *Legion and the Gadarene Swine*, but that must have been because of something faulty in our make-up. The sound of this great anthem was sufficiently impressive to make one long to hear the real Coalition shouting it all along Downing Street. It is a solo with chorus, you understand, and the Coalition come in with a great roar of excitement and fervour on *Doo-dah! Doo-dah!*

Yes, I like that.

THE ART OF DRAWING

It is commonly said that everybody can sing in the bathroom; and this is true. Singing is very easy. Drawing, though, is much more difficult. I have devoted a good deal of time to Drawing, one way and another; I have to attend a great many committees and public meetings, and at such functions I find that Drawing is almost the only Art one can satisfactorily pursue during the speeches. One can seldom sing during the speeches; so as a rule I draw. I do not say that I am an expert yet, but after a few more meetings I calculate that I shall know Drawing as well as it can be known.

The first thing, of course, is to get on to a really good committee; and by a good committee I mean a committee that provides decent materials. An ordinary departmental committee is no use: generally they only give you a couple of pages of lined foolscap and no white blotting paper, and very often the pencils are quite soft. White blotting paper is essential. I know of no material the spoiling of which gives so much artistic pleasure – except perhaps snow. Indeed, if I was asked to choose between making pencil marks on a sheet of white blotting paper and making footmarks on a sheet of white snow I should be in a quandary.

Much the best committees from the point of view of material are committees about business which meet at business premises – shipping offices, for choice. One of the Pacific Lines has the best white blotting paper I know; and the pencils there are a dream. I am sure the directors of that firm are Drawers; for they always give you two pencils, one hard for doing noses, and one soft for doing hair.

When you have selected your committee and the speeches are well away, the Drawing begins. Much the best thing to draw is a man. Not the chairman, or Lord Pommery Quint, or any member of the committee, but just A Man. Many novices make the mistake of selecting a subject for their Art before they begin. Usually they select the chairman; and when they find it is more like Mr Gladstone they are discouraged. If they had waited a little it could have been Mr Gladstone officially. As a rule I begin with the forehead and work down to the chin (Fig. 1).

Fig. 1

When I have done the outline I put in the eye. This is one of the most difficult parts of Drawing; one is never quite sure where the eye goes. If, however, it is not a good eye, a useful tip is to give the man spectacles; this generally makes him a clergyman, but it helps the eye (Fig. 2).

Now you have to outline the rest of the head, and this is rather a gamble. Personally, I go in for *strong* heads (Fig. 3).

I am afraid it is not a strong neck; I expect he is an author, and is not well fed.

Fig. 2

But that is the worst of strong heads; they make it so difficult to join up the chin and the back of the neck.

The next thing to do is to put in the ear; and once you have done this the rest is easy. Ears are much more difficult than eyes (Fig. 4).

I hope that is right. It seems to me to be a little too far to the southward. But it is done now. And once you have put in the ear you can't go back: not unless you are on a *very* good committee which provides india rubber as well as pencils.

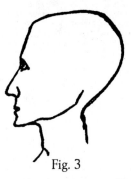

Fig. 3

Now I do the hair. Hair may either be very fuzzy and black, or lightish and thin. It depends chiefly on what sort of pencils are provided. For myself I prefer black hair, because then the parting shows up better (Fig. 5).

Until one draws hair, one never realizes what large heads people have. Doing the hair takes the whole of a speech, usually, even one of the chairman's speeches.

This is not one of my best men; I am sure the ear is in the wrong place. And I am inclined to think he ought to have spectacles. Only then he would be a clergyman, and I have decided that he is Sir Philip Gibbs at the age of twenty. So he must carry on with his eye as it is.

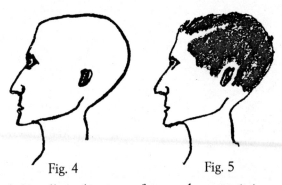

Fig. 4   Fig. 5

I find that all my best men face to the west; it is a curious thing. Sometimes I draw two men facing each other; but the one facing east is never good.

There, you see (Fig. 6)? The one on the right is a Bolshevik; he has a low forehead and beetling brows – a most unpleasant man. Yet he has a powerful face. The one on the left was meant

43

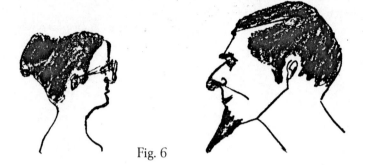

Fig. 6

to be another Bolshevik, arguing with him. But he has turned out to be a lady, so I have had to give her a "bun." She is a lady solicitor; but I don't know how she came to be talking to the Bolshevik.

Here are some more men facing east. They are all a little unconvincing, you see.

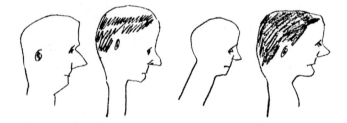

When you have learned how to do Men, the only other things in Drawing are Perspective and Landscape.

Perspective is great fun: the best thing to do is a long French road with telegraph poles (Fig. 7).

I have put in a fence as well. Unstable, I fear.

Landscape is chiefly composed of hills and trees. Trees are the most amusing, especially fluffy trees.

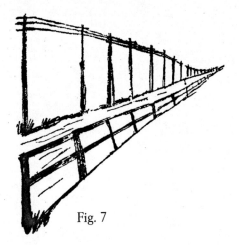

Fig. 7

Here is a Landscape (Fig. 8).

Somehow or other a man has got into this landscape; and, as luck would have it, it is Napoleon. Apart from this it is not a bad one.

But it takes a very long speech to get an ambitious piece of work like this through.

There is one other thing I ought to have said. Never attempt to draw a man front face. It can't be done.

Fig. 8

45

ABOUT BATHROOMS

Of all the beautiful things which are to be seen in shop windows perhaps the most beautiful are those luxurious baths in white enamel, hedged round with attachments and conveniences in burnished metal. Whenever I see one of them I stand and covet it for a long time. Yet even these super baths fall far short of what a bath should be; and as for the perfect bathroom I question if anyone has even imagined it.

The whole attitude of modern civilization to the bathroom is wrong. Why, for one thing, is it always the smallest and barest room in the house? The Romans understood these things; we don't. I have never yet been in a bathroom which was big enough to do my exercises in without either breaking the light or barking my knuckles against a wall. It ought to be a *big* room and opulently furnished. There ought to be pictures in it, so that one could lie back and contemplate them – a picture of troops going up to the trenches, and another picture of a bus queue standing in the rain, and another picture of a windy day with some snow in it. Then one would really enjoy one's baths.

And there ought to be rich rugs in it and profound chairs; one would walk about in bare feet on the rich rugs while the bath was running; and one would sit in the profound chairs while drying the ears.

The fact is, a bathroom ought to be equipped for comfort, like a drawing room, a good, full, velvety room; and as things are it is solely equipped for singing. In the drawing room, where we want to sing, we put so many curtains and carpets and things that most of us can't sing at all; and then we wonder that there is no music in England. Nothing is more maddening than to hear several men refusing to join in a simple chorus after dinner, when you know perfectly well that every one of them has been singing in a high tenor in his bath before dinner. We all know the reason, but we don't take the obvious remedy. The only thing to do is to take all the furniture out of the drawing room and put it in the bathroom – all except the piano and a few cane chairs. Then we shouldn't have those terrible noises in the early morning, and in the evening everybody would be a singer. I suppose that is what they do in Wales.

But if we cannot make the bathroom what it ought to be, the supreme and perfect shrine of the supreme moment of the day, the one spot in the house on which no expense or trouble is spared, we can at least bring the bath itself up to date. I don't now, as I did, lay much stress on having a bath with fifteen different taps. I once stayed in a house with a bath like that. There was a hot tap and a cold tap, and hot sea water and cold sea water, and PLUNGE and SPRAY and SHOWER and WAVE and FLOOD, and one or two more. To turn on the top tap you had to stand on a stepladder, and they were all very highly polished. I was naturally excited by this, and an hour before it was time to dress for dinner I slunk upstairs and hurried into the bathroom and locked myself in and turned on all the taps at once. It was strangely disappointing. The sea water was mythical. Many of the taps refused to function at the same time as any other, and the only two which were really effective were WAVE and FLOOD. WAVE shot out a thin jet of boiling water which caught me in the chest, and FLOOD filled the bath with cold water long before it could be identified and turned off.

No, taps are not of the first importance, though, properly polished, they look well. But no bath is complete without one of those attractive bridges or trays where one puts the sponges and the soap. Conveniences like that are a direct stimulus to

washing. The first time I met one I washed myself all over two or three times simply to make the most of knowing where the soap was. Now and then, in fact, in a sort of bravado I deliberately lost it, so as to be able to catch it again and put it back in full view on the tray. You can also rest your feet on the tray when you are washing them, and so avoid cramp.

Again, I like a bathroom where there is an electric bell just above the bath, which you can ring with the big toe. This is for use when one has gone to sleep in the bath and the water has frozen, or when one has begun to commit suicide and thought better of it. Apart from these two occasions it can be used for Morsing instructions about breakfast to the cook – supposing you have a cook. And if you haven't a cook a little bell ringing in the basement does no harm.

But the most extraordinary thing about the modern bath is that there is no provision for shaving in it. Shaving in the bath I regard as the last word in systematic luxury. But in the ordinary bath it is very difficult. There is nowhere to put anything. There ought to be a kind of shaving tray attached to every bath, which you could swing in on a flexible arm, complete with mirror and soap and strop, new blades and shaving papers and all the other confounded paraphernalia. Then, I think, shaving would be almost tolerable, and there wouldn't be so many of these horrible beards about.

The same applies to smoking. It is incredible that today in the twentieth century there should be no recognised way of disposing of a cigarette end in the bath. Personally I only smoke pipes in the bath, but it is impossible to find a place in which to deposit even a pipe so that it will not roll off into the water. But I have a brother-in-law who smokes cigars in the bath, a disgusting habit. I have often wondered where he hid the ends, and I find now that he has made a *cache* of them in the gas ring of the geyser. One day the ash will get into the burners and then the geyser will explode.

Next door to the shaving and smoking tray should be the book rest. I don't myself do much reading in the bath, but I have several sisters-in-law who keep on coming to stay, and they all do it. Few things make the leaves of a book stick together so easily as being dropped in a hot bath, so they had better have a book rest; and if they go to sleep I shall set in motion my emergency waste mechanism, by which the bath can be emptied in malice from outside.

Another of my inventions is the Progress Indicator. It works like the indicators outside lifts, which show where the lift is and what it is doing. My machine shows what stage the man inside has reached – the washing stage or the merely wallowing stage, or the drying stage, or the exercises stage. It shows you at a glance whether it is worthwhile to go back to bed or whether it is time to dig yourself in on the mat. The machine is specially suitable for hotels and large country houses where you can't find out by hammering on the door and asking, because nobody takes any notice.

When you have properly fitted out the bathroom on these lines all that remains is to put the telephone in and have your meals there; or rather to have your meals there and not put the

"The Progress Indicator."

telephone in. It must still remain the one room where a man is safe from that.

A CRIMINAL TYPE

Today I am MAKing aN inno6£vation. as you mayalready have gessed, I am typlng this article myself Zz^1/$_2$1nstead of writing it, The idea is to save time and exvBKpense, also to demonstyap demonBTrike = = damn, to demonstratO that I can type /ust as well as any blessedgirl if I give my mInd to iT"" Typ1ng while you compose is realy extraoraordinarrily easy, though composing whilr you typE is more difficult. I rather think my typing style is going to be different froM my u6sual style, but Idaresay noone will mind that much. looking back i see that we made rather a hash of that awfuul wurd extraorordinnaryk ? in the middle of a woRd like thaton N-e gets quite lost? 2hy do I keep putting questionmarks instead of fulstopSI wonder. Now you see i have put a fulllstop instead Of a question mark it nevvvver reins but it pours.

the typewriter to me has always been a mustery£? and even now that I have gained a perfect mastery over the machine in gront of me i have npt th3 faintest idea hoW it workss% &or instance why does the thingonthetop the klnd of overhead Wailway arrangement move along one pace afterr every word; I haVe exam aaa ined the mechanism from all points of view but there seeems to be noreason atall whyit shouould do t£is damn that £, it keeps butting in: it is Just lik real life. then there are all kinds oF attractive devisesand levers andbuttons of which is amanvel in itself, and does somethI5g useful without lettin on how it does iT.

Forinstance on this machinE which is Ami/et a mijge7 imean a mi/dgt, made of alumium,, and very light sothat you caN CARRY it about on your £olidays (there is that £ again) and typeout your poems onthe Moon immmmediately, and there is onely one lot of keys for capITals and ordinay latters; when you want todoa Capital you press down a special key marked cap i mean CAP with the lefft hand and yo7 press down the letter withthe other, like that abcd, no, ABCDEFG . how jolly that looks as a mattr of fact th is takes a little gettingintoas all the letters on the keys are printed incapitals so now and then one forgets topress downthe SPecial capit al key. not often, though. on the other hand onceone £as got it down and has written anice nam e in capitals like LLOYdgeORGE IT IS VERY DIFFICULT TO REmemBER TO PUT IT DOWN AGAIN ANDTHE N YOU GET THIS SORT OF THING WHICH SPOILS THE LOOOK OF THE HOLE PAGE . or els insted of preSSing down the key marked CAP onepresses down the key m arked FIG and then instead of LLOYDGEORGE you find that you have written $^1/_2{}^1/_296\%$: 394:3. this is very dissheartcning and £t is no wonder that typists are sooften sououred in ther youth.

Apart fromthat though the key marked FIG is rather fun , since you can rite such amusing things withit, things like % and @ and dear old & not to mention = and $^1/_4$ and $^3/_4$ and !!! i find that inones ordinarry (i never get that word right) cor orrespanden£c one doesnt use expressions like @ @ and %%% nearly enough. typewriting gives you a new ideaof possibilities o fthe engli£h language; thE more i look at % the more beautiful it seems to Be: and like the simple flowers of england itis per£aps most beauti£ul when seeen in the masss, Look atit

%	%	%	%	%	%	%	%	%	%	%	%
%	%	%	%	%	%	%	%	%	%	%	%
%	%	%	%	%	%	%	%	%	%	%	%
%	%	%	%	%	%	%	%	%	%	%	%
%	%	%	%	%	%	%	%	%	%	%	%

how would thatdo for a BAThrooM wallpaper? it could be produced verery cheaply and itcould be calld the CHERRYdesigN damn, imeant to put all that in capitals. iam afraid this articleis spoilt now but butt bUt curse. But perhaps the most excitingthing a£out this mac£ine is that you can by presssing alittle switch suddenly writein redor green instead of in black; I donvt understanh how £t is done butit is very jollY ? busisisness men us e the device a great deal wen writing to their membersof PARLIAment, in order to emphasasise the pointin wich the£r in£ustice is worSe than anyone elses in£ustice . wen they come to WE ARE RUINED they burst out into red and wen they come to WE w WOULD remIND YOU tHAT ATtHE LAST E£ECTION yoU UNDERTOOk they burst into GReeN. thei r typists must enjoy doing those letters. with this arrang ment of corse one coul d do allkinds of capital wallpapers. for lnstance wat about a scheme of red £'s and black %'s and gReen &'s? this sort of thing

£ % £ % £ % £ % £ %
& £ & £ & £ & £ & £
£ % £ % £ % £ % £ %
& £ & £ & £ & £ & £

Manya poor man would be glad to £ave that in his parLour ratherthan wat he has got now. of corse, you wont be ab?e to apreciate the fulll bauty of the design since i underst and that the retched paper which is going to print this has no redink and no green inq either; so you must £ust immagine that the £'s are red and the &'s are green. it is extroarordinarry (wat a t erribleword!!!) how backward in MAny waYs these uptodate papers are wwww $^{1}/4^{1}/4^{1}/4^{1}/4^{1}/4^{1}/4^{1}/2 = {}^{3}/4$ now how did that happen i wond er; i was experimenting with the BACK SPACE key; if that is wat it is for i dont thinq i shall use it again. iI wonder if i am impriving at this$^{1}/2$ sometimes i thinq i am and so metimes i thinq iam not. we have not had so many £'s lately but i notice that theere have been one or two misplaced q's & icannot remember to write i in capital s there it goes again.

Of curse the typewriter, itself is not wolly giltless $^{1}/_{2}$ike all mac&ines it has amind of it sown and is of like passsions with ourselves. i could put that into greek if only the machine was not so hopelessly MOdern. it's chief failing is that it cannot write m'sdecently and instead of h it will keep putting that confounded £. as amatter of fact ithas been doing m's rather

"If i commit a murder."

better today butthat is only its cusssedusssedness and because i
have been opening my shoul ders wenever we have come to an
m; or should it be A m? who can tell; little peculiuliarities like
making indifferent m's are very important & w£en one is bying
a typewriter one s£ould make careful enquiries about themc;
because it is things of that sort wich so often give criminals
away. there is notHing a detective likes so much as a type riter
with an idiosxz an idioynq damit an idiotyncrasy . for instance
if i commit a murder i s£ould not thinq of writing a litter about
it with this of all typewriters becusa because that fool ofa £
would give me away at once I daresay scotland Yard have got
specimens of my trypewriting locked up in some pigeon-hole
allready. if they £avent they ought to; it ought to be part of my
dosossier.

i thing the place of the hypewriter in ART is inshufficiently
apreciated. Modern art i understand is chiefly sumbolical
expression and straigt lines. a typwritr can do strait lines with
the under lining mark) and there are few more atractive
symbols thaN the symbols i have used in this articel ; i merely
thro out the sugestion

I dont tink i shal do many more articles like this it is tooo
much like work ? but I am glad I have got out of that £ habit ;

A P £

THE ART OF POETRY

I

Many people have said to me, "I wish I could write poems. I often try, but – " They mean, I gather, that the impulse, the creative itch, is in them, but they don't know how to satisfy it. My own position is that I know how to write poetry, but I can't be bothered. I have not got the itch. The least I can do, however, is to try to help those who have.

A mistake commonly committed by novices is to make up their minds what it is they are going to say before they begin. This is superfluous effort, tending to cramp the style. It is permissible, if not essential, to select a *subject* – say, MUD – but any detailed argument or plan which may restrict the free development of metre and rhyme (if any) is to be discouraged.

With that understanding, let us now write a poem about MUD.

I should begin in this sort of way:

> Mud, mud,
> Nothing but mud,
> O my God!

It will be seen at once that we are not going to have much rhyme in this poem; or if we do we shall very soon be compelled to strike a sinister note, because almost the only rhymes to mud are *blood* and *flood*; while, as the authors of our

"I often try, but — "

hymns have discovered, there are very few satisfactory rhymes to *God*. They shamefully evaded the difficulty by using words like *road*, but in first-class poetry one cannot do that.

On the whole, therefore, this poem had better be *vers libre*. That will take much less time and be more dramatic, without plunging us into a flood of blood or anything drastic like that. We now go on with a little descriptive business:

> Into the sunset, swallowing up the sun,
> Crawling, creeping,
> The naked flats –

Now there ought to be a verb. That is the worst of *vers libre*; one gets carried away by beautiful phrases and is brought up suddenly by a complete absence of verbs. However at a pinch one can do without a verb; that is the best of *vers libre*:

> Amber and gold,
> Deep-stained in mystery
> And the colours of mystery,
>   Inapprehensible,
> Golden like wet-gold,
> Amber like a woman of Arabia
> That has in her breast
> The forsaken treasures of old Time,
> Love and Destruction,
> Oblivion and Decay,
> And immemorial tins,
>   Tin upon tin,
> Old boots and bottles that hold no more
> Their richness in them.
>   And I –

We might do a good deal more of this descriptive business, bringing in something about dead bodies, mud of course being full of dead bodies. But we had better get on. We strike now the personal note:

> And I,
> I too am no more than a bottle,
>   An empty bottle,
> Heaving helpless on the mud of life,
> Without a label and without a cork,
> Empty I am, yet no man troubles
>   To return me.
>   And why?
> Because there is not sixpence on me.

Bah!
The sun goes down,
  The birds wheel home,
But I remain here,
Drifting empty under the night,
  Drifting –

When one is well away with this part of the poem it is almost impossible to stop. When you are writing in metre you come eventually to the eighth line of the last verse and you have to stop; but in *vers libre* you have no assistance of that kind. This particular poem is being written for instructional purposes in a journal of limited capacity, so it will probably have to stop fairly soon; but in practice it would go on for a long time yet. In any case, however, it would end in the same way, like this:

Mud, mud,
Nothing but mud,
O, my God!

That reasserts, you see, in a striking manner, the original *motif*, and somehow expresses in a few words the poignant melancholy of the whole poem. Another advantage in finishing a long poem, such as this would be, in the same way as you began it is that it makes it clear to the reader that he is still reading the same poem. Sometimes, and especially in *vers libre* of an emotional and digressive character, the reader has a hideous fear that he has turned over two pages and got into another poem altogether. This little trick reassures him; and if you are writing *vers libre* you must not lose any legitimate opportunity of reassuring the reader.

To treat the same theme in metre and rhyme will be a much more difficult matter. The great thing will be to avoid having *mud* at the end of a line, for the reasons already given. We had better have long ten-syllable lines, and we had better have four of them in each verse. Gray wrote an elegy in that metre which has given general satisfaction. We will begin:

> As I came down through Chintonbury Hole
> The tide rolled out from Wurzel to the sea.

In a serious poem of this kind it is essential to establish a locality atmosphere at once; therefore one mentions a few places by name to show that one has been there. If the reader has been there too he will like the poem, and if he hasn't no harm is done. The only thing is that locally Chintonbury is probably pronounced Chun'bury, in which case it will not scan. One cannot be too careful about that sort of thing. However, as an illustration Chintonbury will serve.

It is now necessary to show somehow in this verse that the poem is about mud; it is also necessary to organize a rhyme for "Hole" and a rhyme for "sea," and of the two this is the more important. I shall do it like this:

> And like the unclothéd levels of my soul
> The yellow mud lay mourning nakedly.

There is a good deal to be said against these two lines. For one thing I am not sure that the mud ought to be yellow; it will remind people of Covent Garden Tube Station, and no one wants to be reminded of that. However, it does suggest the inexpressible biliousness of the theme.

I think "levels" is a little weak. It is a good poetical word and doesn't mean anything in particular; but we have too many words of that kind in this verse. "Deserts" would do, except that deserts and mud don't go very well together. However, that sort of point must be left to the individual writer.

At first sight the student may think that "naked*ly*" is not a good rhyme for "sea." Nor is it. If you do that kind of thing in comic poetry no Editor will give you money. But in serious poetry it is quite legitimate; in fact it is rather encouraged. That is why serious poetry is so much easier than comic poetry. In my next lecture I shall deal with comic poetry.

I don't think I shall finish this poem now. The fact is, I am not feeling so inspired as I was. It is very hot. Besides, I have got hay fever and keep on sneezing. Constant sneezing knocks all the inspiration out of a man. At the same time a tendency to hay fever is a sign of intellect and culture, and all the great poets were martyrs to it. That is why none of them grew very lyrical about hay. Corn excited them a good deal, and even straw, but hay hardly ever.

So the student must finish this poem as best he can, and I shall be glad to consider and criticize what he does, though I may say at once that there will be no prize. It ought to go on for another eight verses or so, though that is not essential in these days, for if it simply won't go on it can just stop in the middle. Only then it must be headed "MUD: A Fragment."

And in any case, in the bottom left-hand corner, the student must write:

Chintonbury, May 28th, 1920.

II

In this lecture I propose to explain how comic poetry is written.

Comic poetry, as I think I pointed out in my last lecture, is much more difficult than serious poetry, because there are all sorts of rules. In serious poetry there are practically no rules, and what rules there are may be shattered with impunity as soon as they become at all inconvenient. Rhyme, for instance. A well-known Irish poet once wrote a poem which ran like this:

> "Hands, do as you're bid,
> Draw the balloon of the mind
> That bellies and sags in the wind
> Into its narrow shed."

This was printed in a serious paper; but if the poet had sent it up to a humorous paper (as he might well have done) the Editor would have said, "Do you pronounce it *shid*?" and the poet would have had no answer. You see, he started out, as serious poets do, with every intention of organizing a good rhyme for *bid* – or perhaps for *shed* – but he found this was more difficult than he expected. And then, no doubt, somebody drove all his cattle on to his croquet lawn, or somebody else's croquet lawn, and he abandoned the struggle. I shouldn't complain of that; what I do complain of is the *deceitfulness* of the whole thing. If a man can't find a better rhyme than *shed* for a simple word like *bid*, let him give up the idea of having a rhyme at all; let him write –

> Hands, do as you're TOLD,

or

> Into its narrow HUT (or even HANGAR).

That at least would be an honest confession of failure. But to write *bid* and *shed* is simply a sinister attempt to gain credit for writing a rhymed poem *without doing it at all*.

Well, that kind of thing is not allowed in comic poetry. When I opened my well-known military epic, "Riddles of the King," with the couplet –

> Full dress (with decorations) will be worn
> When General Officers are shot at dawn.

the Editor wrote cuttingly in the margin, "Do you say *dorn*?"

The correct answer would have been, of course, "Well, as a matter of fact I do"; but you cannot make answers of that kind to Editors; they don't understand it. And that brings you to the real drawback of comic poetry; it means constant truck with Editors. But I must not be drawn into a discussion about them. In a special lecture – two special lectures – Quite.

The lowest form of comic poetry is, of course, the Limerick; but it is a mistake to suppose that it is the easiest. It is more difficult to finish a Limerick than to finish anything in the world. You see, in a Limerick you cannot begin:

> There was an old man of West *Ham*

and go on

> Who formed an original *plan*,

finishing the last line with *limb* or *hen* or *bun*. A serious writer could do that with impunity, and indeed with praise, but the more exacting traditions of Limerical composition insist that, having fixed on *Ham* as the end of the first line, you must find two other rhymes to *Ham*, and good rhymes too. This is why there is so large a body of uncompleted Limericks. For many years I have been trying to finish the following unfinished masterpiece:

> There was a young man who said "*Hell!*
> I don't think I feel very well – "

That was composed on the Gallipoli Peninsula; in fact it was composed under fire; indeed I remember now that we were going over the top at the time. But in the quiet days of Peace I can get no further with it. It only shows how much easier it is to begin a Limerick than to end it.

Apart from the subtle phrasing of the second line this poem is noteworthy because it is cast in the classic form. All the best Limericks are about a young man, or else an old one, who said some short sharp monosyllable in the first line. For example:

> There was a young man who said "*If –*

Now what are the rhymes to *if*? Looking up my *Rhyming Dictionary* I see they are:

cliff	hieroglyph	hippogriff
skiff	sniff stiff	tiff whiff

Of these one may reject *hippogriff* at once, as it is in the wrong metre. *Hieroglyph* is attractive, and we might do worse than:

> There was a young man who said "If
> One murdered a hieroglyph – "

Having, however, no very clear idea of the nature of a hieroglyph I am afraid that this will also join the long list of unfinished masterpieces. Personally I should incline to something of this kind:

> There was a young man who said "If
> I threw myself over a cliff
>   I do not believe
>   *One* person would grieve – "

Now the last line is going to be very difficult. The tragic loneliness, the utter disillusion of this young man is so vividly outlined in the first part of the poem that to avoid an anticlimax a really powerful last line is required. *But there are no powerful rhymes.* A serious poet, of course, could finish up with *death* or *faith*, or some powerful word like that. But we are limited to *skiff, sniff, tiff* and *whiff.* And what can you do with those? Students, I hope, will see what they can do. My own tentative solution is printed, by arrangement with the Publisher, on another page (84)*. I do not pretend that it is perfect; in fact it seems to me to strike rather a vulgar note. At the same time it is copyright, and must not be set to music in the USA.

* SOLUTION: It comes of my having a sniff.

"There was a young man who said 'If'."

I have left little time for comic poetry other than Limericks, but most of the above profound observations are equally applicable to both, except that in the case of the former it is usual to think of the *last* line first. Having done that you think of some good rhymes to the last line and hang them up in mid-air, so to speak. Then you think of something to say which will fit on to those rhymes. It is just like Limericks, only you start at the other end; indeed it is much easier than Limericks, though, I am glad to say, nobody believes this. If they did it would be even harder to get money out of Editors than it is already.

We will now write a comic poem about Spring Cleaning. We will have verses of six lines, five ten-syllable lines and one six-syllable. As a last line for the first verse I suggest

Where have they put my hat?

We now require two rhymes to *hat*. In the present context *flat* will obviously be one, and *cat* or *drat* will be another. Our resources at present are therefore as follows:

Line   1 ———
   "   2 – … flat.
   "   3 – –
   "   4 – … cat or drat.
   "   5 – –
   "   6 – Where have they put my hat?

As for the blank lines, *wife* is certain to come in sooner or later, and we had better put that down, supported by *life* ("What a life!"), and *knife* or *strife*. There are no other rhymes, except *rife*, which is a useless word.

We now hold another parade:

Terumti – umti – umti – umti – wife,
   Terumti – umti – umti – umti – flat;
Teroodle – oodle – oodle – What a life!
   Terumti – oodle – umti – oodle – cat (or drat);
Teroodle – umti – oodle – umti – knife (or strife);
   Where have they put my hat?

All that remains now is to fill in the umti-oodles, and I can't be bothered to do that. There is nothing in it.

"Where have they put my hat?"

III

In this lecture I shall deal with the production of Lyrics, Blank Verse and (if I am allowed) Hymns (Ancient and Modern).

First we will write a humorous lyric for the Stage, bearing in mind, of course, the peculiar foibles, idiosyncrasies and whims of Mr Alf Bubble, who will sing it (we hope). Mr Bubble's principal source of fun is the personal appearance of his fellow-citizens. Whenever a new character comes on the stage he makes some remark about the character's "face." Whenever he does this the entire audience rolls about on its seat, and cackles and gurgles and wipes its eyes, and repeats in a hoarse whisper, with variations of its own, the uproarious phrasing of Mr Bubble's remark. If Mr Bubble says, "But look at his *face!*" the audience, fearful lest its neighbours may have missed the cream of the thing, splutters hysterically in the intervals of eye-wiping and coughing and choking and sneezing, "He said, '*What* a face!'" or "He said, '*Did* you *see* his face?'" or "He said, 'Is it a *face?*'"

All this we have got to remember when we are writing a lyric for Mr Bubble. Why Mr Bubble of all people should find so much mirth in other men's faces I can't say, but there it is. If we write a song embodying this great joke we may be certain that it will please Mr Bubble; so we will do it.

Somebody, I think, will have made some slighting remark about the Government, and that will give the cue for the first verse, which will be political.

We will begin:

Thompson...

I don't know why the people in humorous lyrics are always called Thompson (or Brown), but they are.

Thompson, being indigent,
Thought that it was time he went
Into England's Parliament,
    To earn his daily bread...

That is a joke against Parliament, you see – Payment of Members and all that; it is good. At the same time it is usual to reserve one's jokes for the chorus. The composer, you see,

"They all get ready to burst themselves."

68

reserves his tune for the chorus, and, if the author puts too much into the verse, there will be trouble between their Unions.

Now we introduce the *face-motif*:

> Thompson's features were not neat;
> When he canvassed dahn our street
> Things were said I won't repeat,
>   And my old moth-ah said:

This verse, you notice, is both in metre and rhyme; I don't know how that has happened; it ought not to be.

Now we have the chorus:

> "Oh, Mr Thompson,
>   It isn't any good;
> I shouldn't like to vote for you,
>   So I won't pretend I should;
> I know that you're the noblest
>   Of all the human race..."

That shows the audience that *face* is coming very soon, and they all get ready to burst themselves.

> "I haven't a doubt, if you get in,
> The Golden Age will soon begin –
>   But I DON'T LIKE – your FACE."

At this point several of the audience will simply slide off their seats on to the floor, and wallow about there, snorting.

The next verse had better be a love verse.

> Thompson wooed a lovely maid
> Every evening in the shade,
> Meaning, I am much afraid,

To hide his ugly head…

Head is not very good, I admit, but we must have said in the last line, and as we were mad enough to have rhymes in the first verse we have got to go on with it.

But when he proposed one night –
Did it by electric light –
Mabel, who retained her sight,
    Just looked at him and said:

Now you see the idea?

"Oh, Mr Thompson,
    It isn't any good;
I shouldn't like to marry you,
    So I won't pretend I should;
I know that you have riches
    And a house in Eaton Place…

(Here all the audience pulls out its handkerchief)

I haven't a doubt that you must be
The properest possible match for me,
    But I DON'T LIKE – your FACE."

I have got another verse to this song, but I will not give it to you now, as I think the Editor is rather bored with it. It is fortunate for Mr Bubble that he does not have to perform before an audience of Editors.

Having written the lyric the next thing to do is to get a composer to compose music for it, and then you get it published. This is most difficult, as composers are people who don't ever keep appointments, and music publishers like locking up lyrics in drawers till the mice have got at the chorus and the whole thing is out of date.

By the time that this song is ready Mr Bubble may quite possibly have exhausted the *face-motif* altogether and struck a new vein. Then we shall have wasted our labour. In that case we will arrange to have it buried in somebody's grave (Mr Bubble's for choice), and in AD 2000 it will be dug up by antiquaries and deciphered. Even a lyric like this may become an Old Manuscript in time. I ought to add that I myself have composed the music for this lyric, but I really cannot undertake to explain composing as well as poetry.

The serious lyric or Queen's Hall ballad is a much easier affair. But I must first warn the student that there are some peculiar customs attaching to this traffic which may at first sight appear discouraging. When you have written a good lyric and induced someone to compose a tune for it your first

"Mr Throstle… will expect to be paid about fifty pounds."

thought will be, "I will get Mr Throstle to sing this, and he will pay me a small fee or royalty per performance"; and this indeed would be a good arrangement to make. The only objection is that Mr Throstle, so far from paying any money to the student, will expect to be paid about fifty pounds by the student for singing his lyric. I do not know the origin of this quaint old custom, but the student had better not borrow any money on the security of his first lyric.

For a serious or Queen's Hall lyric all that is necessary is to think of some natural objects like the sun, the birds, the flowers or the trees, mention them briefly in the first verse and then in the second verse draw a sort of analogy or comparison between the natural object and something to do with love. The verses can be extremely short, since in this class of music the composer is allowed to spread himself and can indefinitely eke out the tiniest words.

Here is a perfect lyric I have written. It is called, quite simply, *Evening:*

> Sunshine in the forest,
>   Blossom on the tree,
> And all the brave birds singing
>   For you – and me.
>
> Kisses in the sunshine,
>   Laughter in the dew,
> And all the brave world singing
>   For me – and you.

I see now that the dew has got into the second verse, so it had better be called quite simply "The Dawn."

You notice the artistic parallelism of this lyric; I mean, "The brave birds singing" in one verse and "The brave *world* singing" in the next. That is a tip I got from Hebrew poetry, especially the Psalms: "One day telleth another; and one night certifieth another," and so on. It is a useful trick to remember, and is employed freely by many modern writers, the author of

"The King's Regulations," for example, who in Regulation 1680 has the fine line:

"Disembarkations are carried out in a similar manner to embarkations."

That goes well to the Chant in C major by Mr P Humphreys.

But I am wandering. It is becoming clear to me now that I shall not have time to do Blank Verse or Hymns (Ancient and Modern) in this lecture, after all, so I will give you a rough outline of that special kind of lyric, the Topical Song. All that is required for this class of work is a good refrain or central idea; when you have got that, you see how many topics you can tack on to it. But if you can tack on Mr Winston Churchill you need not bother about the others.

Our central idea will be "Rations," and the song will be called "Heaps and Heaps":

Now Jimmy Brown

(always begin like that)

Now Jimmy Brown
He went to town,
But all the people said,
"We're rationed in our jam, you know,
Likewise our cheese and bread;

But we've lots of politicians
And Ministers galore,
We've got enough of them and, gee!
We don't want any more."

Chorus.

We've had heaps and heaps and heaps of Mr SMILLIE (Loud
   cheers.);
   We've had heaps and heaps and heaps of our MP
      (Significant chuckles);
         At political carouses
      We've had heaps of (paper) houses
   But though we WAIT, no houses do we SEE (Bitter laughter).
The khaki-boys were good enough for fighting,
   But now we hear the khaki-coat is barred;
If they ration us in Mr WINSTON CHURCHILL,
   Why, anyone may have my ration-card! (Uproar.)

All you have to do now is to work in some more topics. I
don't think I shall do any more now. The truth is that that verse
has rather taken it out of me.
   I feel all barren.

THE BOOK OF JONAH

(As almost any modern Irishman would have written it)

(The circumlocution of the play – there is no action – takes place I don't know where and I can't think when. But the scene is the corner of the village square. Mrs Joner is discovered sitting in front of her house, knitting, washing socks, or perhaps just thinking. In the distance can be seen the figure of a male statue, very new, with a long inscription on the pedestal. Timothy James O'Leary walks by, gazing at the statue.)

T.J. Good day to you, Bridget Ellen Joner. And it's many's the day since I was seeing you. *(With a jerk of his head.)* And isn't it the fine statue you have on himself there?

Mrs J. It is so. Though, indeed, it is like no husband I ever had – or ever will have, I'm hoping.

TJ. It is not – and why would it be? Who wants likenesses in a statue when they have all that writing and printing below to tell who it is above – (*piously*) – "Michael Flannigan Joner, that gave his life for his fellow-travellers"?

Mrs J. Aye, it was the only time he ever gave anything away in my life, to my knowing, unless it would be them sermons and prophecies that he would be handing to the folk in the public street, and none wanting them any more than the cows in the bog.

TJ. Ah, it was a queer thing entirely! Have you heard any more now what was the way of it, for I am not understanding how it was at all.

Mrs J. It was the sailors of the ship that did be saying they would sail the ship no longer when they found that himself was in the Post Office, and him travelling for the Government. And there was a great storm and the ship tossing the way you wouldn't know was she a ship at all, or a cork that a boy throws in the water out of a bottle; and the sailors said it was the English Government – and why would it not be? – and they cried out against himself and said it was having the ship sunk on them he would be, and he rose up out of his bed and "Is it sinking the ship I would be?" he said, and he threw himself over the side into the water – and that was the way of it.

TJ (reflectively). And him with the rheumatics – God rest his soul! And have you any pension taken from the Government?

Mrs J. I have so. And it's worth more to me he is now he's dead than ever he was when he was alive with all his praying and preaching and prophesying –

TJ. Maybe it's thinking of marrying again you might be?

Mrs J. And how would I be marrying again, Timothy James, and I a lone widow woman with no money to pay for the roof over my head – let alone weddings?

T.J. And why would you not be? Sure, you have the pension for himself, and what better use can a woman find for a pension that is for her man that is dead than to get another that is alive and well?

Mrs J. Will you tell me now where I would find a husband that would be the equal of a man who gave his life for his fellow-travellers – and him with the rheumatics?

T.J. Sure, it's the grand position you have entirely now, and every man and woman in the whole countryside scheming and scraping to give a few pennies to the collection for the statue, and the Lord Lieutenant himself coming down for the unveiling – and it's difficult it would be to find a man that was fine

"Michael Flannigan Joner."

enough to marry you at all – but – but (*looking round*) don't I know the very man for you?

Mrs J. And who might that be, for goodness sake?

TJ (*confidentially*). Come within now and I'll tell you. I'd be fearful here that one of the lads would maybe hear me.

Mrs J (*with brief reluctance*). Come within then.

(*They go into the house.*)

(*A man strolls along the road, looking about him with keen interest; he is wild and mysterious of aspect, with shaggy hair and travel-stained, untidy clothes. He stops with a start in front of the statue and gazes at it with amazement; then he slowly reads the inscription.*)

Mr J. "Michael Flannigan Joner, who gave his life for his fellow-travellers." (*In stupefaction.*) Glory be to God! (*Turning to the house.*) Bridget Ellen – are you within there? (*He turns and gazes at the statue again.*)

(*There is a sound of laughter in the house. Mrs J and Timothy J come out, arm-in-arm and affectionate: they see the man and stop dead in the doorway.*)

TJ. Glory be to God!

Mrs J. The Saints preserve us!

TJ. If it isn't Michael Joner himself!

Mr J. It is so (*pointing indignantly*). And what call had you to make a graven image of him in the public street the like of the Kings of England or Parnell himself?

Mrs J. And what call had you to come back from the dead without a word of warning and I after promising myself to a better man?

Mr J (*still full of the statue*). "Gave his life for his fellow-trav—" And is it mad you all are?

Mrs J. Then you did not so? (*To TJ*) Wasn't I telling you?

Mr J. I did not indeed. And why would I – the low heathen – and I that had my fare paid to Tarshish?

Mrs J and TJ raise their eyebrows at this suspicious utterance.

Mrs J. Tarshish! Sure it's drunk he is!… Then how came you lepping into the water like a young dog or a boy that does be diving in the hot weather, and you with –

Mr J. It was not lepping I was nor diving neither, but it's thrown in I was by a lot of heathen sailors because I was after prophesying the wrath of the Lord upon them –

Mrs J. Didn't I tell you now that no good would come of the prophesying, and you that was brought up a decent lad by your own father in Kilbay?

TJ. And what happened to you when you were thrown in at all?

Mr J. Sure, I was swallowed by a great whale, and the Lord said to the whale –

TJ. Holy Mother! It's mad he is and not drunk at all!

Mr J. It is not mad I am nor drunk either. Wasn't I three days and three nights in the belly of the whale, and the sea roaring without, the same as a man would lie in his warm bed and it raining –

Mrs J. Three days and three nights! – and isn't it nine months since you lepped out of the ship? Will you tell me now where you have been in the meanwhile and what you were doing at all?

Mr J. Sure the Lord spoke to the whale, and the whale threw me up on the dry land –

Mrs J (*suspicious soul*). And where would that be now?

Mr J. Sure I don't know now –

Mrs J. I should think not indeed –

Mr J. – but it was a small little island and devil a ship came there at all to take me away –

Mrs J (*to TJ, lifting her hands*). Did you ever hear the like of that? And were there any fine young ladies or mermaids maybe on that same small little island?

Mr J. There were not then – nor statues either.

TJ (*humouring him*). And what might ye be doing while you were in the belly of the whale, Michael Flannigan?

Mr J. And why wouldn't I be prophesying and praying unto the Lord, the way he would calm the whale, and it roaring and lepping in the sea like a trout that has the hook swallowed, and it tickling…?

Mrs J. It's well you might be praying unto the Lord, Michael Flannigan, for it's a queer thing entirely if a lone widow woman can no more be left in peace without her man coming back from the dead to frighten her out of her wits with whales and the like, the way she would be the laughing stock of the whole countryside! And it's devil a penny will I have from the Government now seeing you are alive again and not dead at all.

T J. It's a true word, Michael Flannigan, and it's queer uneasy I am myself that had set my heart on marrying your own wife.

Mrs J. And will you tell me now what will we be after doing with the grand statue we have put up on you, Michael Flannigan, and it's myself that has the flesh worn from my fingers with working to put a few shillings together to pay for it?

Mr J (infuriated). Is it *I* that was asking for a statue at all? (*He regards it.*) But sure it is a fine thing entirely – and why would it not stay where it is?

Mrs J. And the whole world coming here by the train to make a mock of me, the way they would be seeing the statue of the man who "gave his life for his fellow-travellers," and him sleeping in his own bed all the time like a common man!

Mr J. Common, is it? Is it *every* day you have a man coming from the dead that was three days and three nights in the belly of a whale?

Mrs J. It is not – thanks be to God!

T J. What ails you now, Bridget Ellen! Why wouldn't we be altering the writing that is below the statue and write down this story about the whale, or any other fairy story that he might be thinking of in the night and him lying awake – for sure it is a grand story and I wouldn't wonder would the folk be travelling out from the big towns to see the man that was in the belly of

80

a whale, when they wouldn't walk across the road to see a man that gave his life for his fellow-travellers, and they English as like as not.

Mrs J. It's little the money I'll be getting out of that, I'm thinking.

TJ. And why will you not? It could be that them music halls in the big towns and the theayters themselves would pay money to Michael Flannigan for no more than walking on the stage and telling the people what went on while he was in the whale – the same as they would for a cow that has five legs or the smallest woman in the world. Sure, didn't they give Peter O'Flaherty three pounds for the loan of his duck that had no legs at all?

Mrs J. It could be that they might, Timothy James.

Mr J. There is money in them whales, 'tis true, and they full of whalebone, the same as the fine ladies do use in Dublin for their dress and all. And when I was smoking my tobacco pipe in the whale, the oil did be running down the inside of the creature the way I was afeared he would take fire and the two of us be destroyed altogether.

TJ (admiringly). Did you ever hear the like, of that? There's them at the theayters that would pay you a mint of money for that same story, Michael Flannigan!

Mr J. They might so.

TJ. But tell me now, Michael Flannigan, is it the truth or no that them whales have the queer small throats on them, the way they couldn't swallow a little whiting, let alone a big man? It could be that one of them writing fellows would rise up in the theayter and say there was no man yet was swallowed by a whale, nor will be neither, because of the queer small throat they have on them! How would it be if you were to give it out that you were swallowed by a *big fish*, the way the ignorant folk would guess it was a whale and the people that do understand whales wouldn't be able to say you were telling a lie?

Mr J. 'Tis a great head you have on you, Timothy James, and it's sorry I am it was myself was in the whale and not you.

T.J. Faith, 'tis glad I am I was never in a whale, for they do say they belong to the English King, the creatures, and God knows what may come of the like of that!

Mr J. Is it the King of England's they are? Then, Glory be to God, I'll have no more to do with them!

T.J. Sure, and there's nothing wrong with the King's money, is there? And it's plenty of that there will be, I'm thinking. I tell you, it's the grand story they'll make in the history books till the world's end of Michael Flannigan Joner that was ate by a whale!

Mrs J. And devil a word will they say of Bridget Ellen, his wife, that was married to a mad fellow.

T.J. Let you not be vexing yourself now. I wouldn't wonder would one of them writing fellows be writing a book about you, or maybe a play, and it's the grand talk there will be of Joner's wife at the latter end.

Mrs J. It might.

(CURTAIN)

THE MYSTERY OF THE APPLE-PIE BEDS

(LEAVES FROM A HOLIDAY DIARY)

I

An outrage has occurred in the hotel. Late on Monday night ten innocent visitors discovered themselves the possessors of apple-pie beds. The beds were not of the offensive hairbrush variety, but they were very cleverly constructed, the under sheet being pulled up in the good old way and turned over at the top as if it were the top sheet.

I had one myself. The lights go out at eleven and I got into bed in the dark. When one is very old and has not been to school for a long time or had an apple-pie bed for longer still, there is something very uncanny in the sensation, especially if it is dark. I did not like it at all. My young brother-in-law, Denys, laughed immoderately in the other bed at my flounderings and imprecations. He did not have one. I suspect him…

II

Naturally the hotel is very much excited. It is the most thrilling event since the mixed foursomes. Nothing else has been discussed since breakfast. Ten people had beds and about ten people are suspected. The really extraordinary thing is that numbers of people seem to suspect *me*! That is the worst of being a professional humorist; everything is put down to you. When I was accompanying Mrs F today she suddenly stopped fiddling and said hotly that someone had been tampering with her violin. I know she suspected me. Fortunately, however, I have a very good answer to this apple-pie bed charge. Eric says that his bed must have been done after dinner, and I was to be seen at the dance in the lounge all the evening. I have an alibi.

Besides, I had a bed myself; surely they don't believe that even a professional humorist could be so bursting with humour as to make himself an apple-pie bed and not make one for his brother-in-law in the same room! It would be too much like overtime.

But they say that only shows my cleverness...

III

Then there is the question of the Barkers. Most of the victims were young people, who could not possibly mind. But the Barkers had two, and the Barkers are a respected middle-aged couple, and nobody could possibly make them apple-pie beds who did not know them very well. That shows you it can't have been me – I – me – that shows you I couldn't have done it. I have only spoken to them once.

They say Mr Barker was rather annoyed. He has rheumatism and went to bed early. Mrs Barker discovered about her bed before she got in, but she didn't let on. She put out the candle and allowed her lord to get into his apple-pie in the dark. I think I shall like her.

They couldn't find the matches. I believe he was quite angry...

IV

I suspect Denys and Joan. They are engaged, and people in that state are capable of anything. Neither of them had one, and they were seen slipping upstairs during the dance. They say they went out on the balcony – a pretty story...

V

I suspect the Barkers. You know, that story about Mrs B letting Mr B get into his without warning him was pretty thin. Can you imagine an English wife doing a thing of that kind? If you can it ought to be a ground for divorce under the new Bill. But you can't.

Then all that stuff about the rheumatism – clever but unconvincing. Mr Barker stayed in his room all the next morning *when the awkward questions were being asked*. Not well; oh, no! But he was down for lunch and conducting for a glee party in the drawing room afterwards, as perky and active as a professional. Besides, the really unanswerable problem is, who could have *dared* to make the Barkers' apple-pie beds? And the answer is, nobody – except the Barkers.

And there must have been a lady in it, it was so neatly done. Everybody says no *man* could have done it. So that shows you it couldn't have been me – I…

VI

I suspect Mr Winthrop. Mr Winthrop is fifty-three. He has been in the hotel since this time last year, and he makes accurate forecasts of the weather. My experience is that a man who makes accurate forecasts of the weather may get up to any devilry. And he protests too much. He keeps coming up to me and making long speeches to prove that he didn't do it. But I never said he did. Somebody else started that rumour, but of course he thinks that I did. That comes of being a professional humorist.

But I do believe he did it. You see he is fifty-three and doesn't dance, so he had the whole evening to do it in.

Tonight we are going to have a Court of Inquiry…

VII

We have had the Inquiry. I was judge. I started with Denys and Joan in the dock, as I thought we must have somebody there and it would look better if it was somebody in the family. The first witness was Mrs Barker. Her evidence was so unsatisfactory that I had to have her put in the dock too. So was Mr Barker's. I was sorry to put him in the dock, as he still had rheumatics. But he had to go.

So did Mr Winthrop. I had no qualms about him. For a man of his age to do a thing like that seems to me really deplorable. And the barefaced evasiveness of his evidence! He simply could not account for his movements during the evening at all. When I asked him what he had been doing at 9.21, and where, he actually said he *didn't know*.

Rather curious – very few people *can* account for their movements, or anyone else's. In most criminal trials the witnesses remember to a minute, years after the event, exactly what time they went upstairs and when they passed the prisoner in the lounge, but nobody seems to remember anything in this affair. No doubt it will come in time.

The trial was very realistic. I was able to make one or two excellent judicial jokes. Right at the beginning I said to the prosecuting counsel, "What *is* an apple-pie bed?" and when he had explained I said with a meaning look, "You mean that the bed was not in *apple-pie order?*" Ha, ha! Everybody laughed heartily…

VIII

In my address to the jury of matrons I was able to show pretty clearly that the crime was the work of a gang. I proved that Denys and Joan must have done the bulk of the dirty work, under the tactical direction of the Barkers, who did the rest; while in the background was the sinister figure of Mr Winthrop, the strategical genius, the lurking Macchiavelli of the gang.

The jury were not long in considering their verdict. They said: "We find, your Lordship, that you did it yourself, with some lady or ladies unknown."

That comes of being a professional humorist…

IX

I ignored the verdict. I addressed the prisoners very severely and sentenced them to do the Chasm hole from 6.0 a.m. to 6.0 p.m. every day for a week, to take out cards and play out every stroke. "You, Winthrop," I said, "with your gentlemanly cunning, your subtle pretensions of righteousness – " But there is no space for that…

"The lurking Macchiavelli of the gang."

X

As a matter of fact the jury were quite right. In company with a lady who shall be nameless I did do it. At least, at one time I thought I did. Only we have proved so often that somebody else did it, we have shown so conclusively that we can't have done it, that we find ourselves wondering if we really did.

Perhaps we didn't.

If we did we apologize to all concerned – except, of course, to Mr Winthrop. I suspect him.

THE GRASSHOPPER

The Animal Kingdom may be divided into creatures which one can feed and creatures which one cannot feed. Animals which one· cannot feed are nearly always unsatisfactory; and the grasshopper is no exception. Anyone who has tried feeding a grasshopper will agree with me.

Yet he is one of the most interesting of British creatures. The *Encyclopaedia Britannica* is as terse and simple as ever about him. "Grasshoppers," it says, "are specially remarkable for their saltatory powers, due to the great development of the hind legs; and also for their stridulation, which is not always an attribute of the male only." To translate, grasshoppers have a habit of hopping ("saltatory powers") and chirping ("stridulation").

It is commonly supposed that the grasshopper stridulates by rubbing his back legs together; but this is not the case. For one thing I have tried it myself and failed to make any kind of noise; and for another, after exhaustive observations, I have established the fact that, though he does move his back legs every time he stridulates, *his back legs do not touch each other*. Now it is a law of friction that you cannot have friction between two back legs if the back legs are not touching; in other words the grasshopper does not rub his back legs together to produce stridulation, or, to put it quite shortly, he does not rub his back legs together *at all*. I hope I have made this point quite clear. If not, a more detailed treatment will be found in the Paper which I read to the Royal Society in 1912.

Nevertheless I have always felt that there was something fishy about the grasshopper's back legs. I mean, why *should* he wave his back legs about when he is stridulating? My own theory is that it is purely due to the nervous excitement produced by the act of singing. The same phenomenon can be observed in many singers and public speakers. I do not think myself that we need seek for a more elaborate hypothesis. The *Encyclopaedia Britannica*, of course, says that "the stridulation or song in the *Acridiidae* is produced by friction of the hind legs against portions of the wings or wing-covers," but that is just the sort of statement which the scientific man thinks he can pass off on the public with impunity. Considering that stridulation takes place about every ten seconds, I calculate that the grasshopper must require a new set of wings every ten days. It would be more in keeping with the traditions of our public life if the scientific man simply confessed that he was baffled by this problem of the grasshopper's back legs. Yet, as I have said, if a public speaker may fidget with his back legs while he is stridulating, why not a public grasshopper? The more I see of science the more it strikes me as one large mystification.

But I ought to have mentioned that "the *Acridiidae* have the auditory organs on the first abdominal segment," while "the *Locustidae* have the auditory organ on the *tibia* of the first leg." In other words, one kind of grasshopper hears with its stomach and the other kind listens with its leg. When a scientific man has committed himself to that kind of statement he would hardly have qualms about a little invention like the back-legs legend.

With this scientific preliminary we now come to the really intriguing part of our subject, and that is the place of the grasshopper in modern politics. And the first question is, Why did Mr Lloyd George call Lord Northcliffe a grasshopper? I think it was in a speech about Russia that Mr Lloyd George said, in terms, that Lord Northcliffe was a grasshopper. And he didn't leave it at that. He said that Lord Northcliffe was not only a grasshopper but a something something grasshopper, grasshopping here and grasshopping there – you know the sort of thing. There was nothing much in the accusation, of course, and Lord Northcliffe made no reply at the time; in fact, so far as I know, he has never publicly stated that he is *not* a grasshopper; for all we know it may be true. But I know a man whose wife's sister was in service at a place where there was a kitchen maid whose young man was once a gardener at Lord Northcliffe's, and this man told me – the first man, I mean – that Lord Northcliffe took it to heart terribly. No grasshoppers were allowed in the garden from that day forth; no green that was at all like grasshopper-green was tolerated in the house, and the gardener used to come upon his Lordship muttering in the West Walk: "A grasshopper! He called me a grasshopper – ME – a GRASSHOPPER!" The gardener said that his Lordship used to finish up with, "*I'll* teach him"; but that is hardly the kind of thing a lord would say, and I don't believe it. In fact I don't believe any of it. It is a stupid story.

But this crisis we keep having with France owing to Mr Lloyd George's infamous conduct does make the story interesting. The suggestion is, you see, that Lord Northcliffe lay low for a long time, till everybody had forgotten about the grasshopper and Mr Lloyd George thought that Lord Northcliffe had forgotten about the grasshopper, and then, when Mr Lloyd George was in a hole, Lord Northcliffe said, "*Now* we'll see if I

"He called me a grasshopper – ME – A GRASSHOPPER!"

am a grasshopper or not," and started stridulating at high speed about Mr Lloyd George. A crude suggestion. But if it were true it would mean that the grasshopper had become a figure of national and international importance. It is wonderful to think that we might stop being friends with France just because of a grasshopper; and, if Lord Northcliffe arranged for a new Government to come in, it might very well be called "The Grasshopper Government." That would look fine in the margins of the history books.

Yes, it is all very "dramatic." It is exciting to think of an English lord nursing a grievance about a grasshopper for months and months, seeing grasshoppers in every corner, dreaming about grasshoppers… But we must not waste time over the fantastic tale. We have not yet solved our principal problem. Why did Mr Lloyd George call him a grasshopper – a modest, friendly little grasshopper? Did he mean to suggest that Lord Northcliffe hears with his stomach or stridulates with his back legs?

Why not an earwig, or a black beetle, or a woodlouse, or a centipede? There are lots of insects more offensive than the grasshopper, and personally I would much rather be called a grasshopper than an earwig, which gets into people's sponges and frightens them to death.

Perhaps he had been reading that nice passage in the Prophet Nahum: "Thy captains are as the great grasshoppers, which camp in the hedges in the cold day, but when the sun ariseth they flee away, and their place is not known where they are," or the one in Ecclesiastes: "And the grasshopper shall be a burden." I do not know. On the other hand, the *Encyclopaedia* has a suggestive sentence: "All grasshoppers are vegetable feeders and have an incomplete metamorphosis, so that *their destructive powers are continuous from the moment of emergence from the egg until death.*"

LITTLE BITS OF LONDON

I

THE SUPREME COURT

Among those curious corners of London life which anyone may go to see but nobody does, one of the most curious, and (for about five minutes) interesting, is the House of Lords sitting as the Supreme Court of Appeal. It is one of the ordinary things which go on and on unnoticed for a lifetime because they have gone on so long, till one day one begins to think about them and realizes suddenly that they were really extraordinary all the time – just as one pronounces sometimes with a startling sense of its absurdity some common English word. But no sightseer, no student of our institutions, and particularly no one who is interested in the ways and customs of individual trades, should fail to visit the Supreme Appellate Tribunal of this great country.

The funny thing about the House of Lords sitting as a court is that it actually sits in the House of Lords. Entering the great red chamber – as anybody may do if he can find the way – one receives the impression that it is perfectly empty, save for the knot of barristers' clerks, solicitors' clerks, pressmen and casual onlookers who are huddled round the entrance. Beyond them are miles, and miles, and miles of red leather benches, silent, mournful, untenanted, dead. But no! A low monotonous drone reaches you – like the voice of a priest intoning at the other end of a cathedral. Guided by this sound you discover faint traces of life on one of the vast red benches. There is an old man sitting on the bench, a pleasant, bearded old man; he does not look at all legal, and he is dressed in everyday clothes, huddled up in front of a sort of small card table covered with huge tomes. He is speaking apparently into space – in a kind of squeaky hum, if you can imagine the sound – fumbling all the time with the large brown tomes.

Look again. Beyond him, a very long way off, is another old man, a very, very jolly old man, with another beard, another card table, and more tomes. He is staring with profundity at the bench opposite. Following his gaze, you detect with amazement another old man, all alone on the great red bench. No, not alone. With something of the sensations of a man who stands by a stagnant pond or looks at a drop of drinking water through a microscope to discover that it is teeming with life, you detect yet a fourth old man on the very same bench, though, of course, a long way away. Both of them are equipped as the others, though one of them, for some reason which does not appear, has no beard. You are ready for anything now, so quite quickly you find the fifth old man, far, far away in the distance, all alone on an island in the emptiness, so far off that he seems to be cut off from all communication with the other old men, or anyone else. Yet suddenly his lips move, and it is seen that he is speaking. He is the presiding old man, and he begins speaking while the first old man is still droning. From the faint movement of his head and the far gleam of his eyes you draw the conclusion that he is speaking to some living creature in your own neighbourhood; and, sure enough, you find that close to you, but curtained off, there are seven or eight men shut up in a wooden pen about seven feet square. These must be the prisoners, and that is the dock, you think. But no, it is the barristers; as the House of Lords is very holy they are only allowed to huddle on the doorstep. One of them is standing in front of the pen at a sort of lectern, wearing a vast wig (the special House of Lords wig), and waiting patiently till the old men have stopped squeaking. Most of the other men in the pen are asleep, but two of them are crouching intently behind the other one, and they keep tugging at his gown, or poking him in the back, and whispering suggestions at him. When they do this he whispers back with an aspect of calm, "Yes, yes – I follow," but you know he does not follow, and you know he is really in a great rage, because he is trying to hear with the other ear what the old man is saying, and the old man is so far away and his voice is so gentle, and his sentences are so long and so full of parentheses, very often in Latin, that it is hard enough to have to follow him, without being whispered at from the rear.

At last the old man shuts his mouth very firmly in a legal manner, and it is clear that he has stopped speaking. It is the barrister's turn. He starts off with a huge sentence about "the presumption of intent under the Drains and Mortgages (Consolidation) Act, 1892," but when he is right in the middle of it the fourth old man, whom everybody supposed to be fast asleep, wakes up and asks the barrister an awkward question about the Amending Act of 1899, just to show that he has got a grip of the whole thing. The barrister has not the faintest idea what the answer is, but he begins one immediately, as if it was quite easy, for that is the game. While he is groping about in the middle of a huge remark which means nothing at present but may very likely lead him to the right answer in the end, the third old man, in order to confuse the barrister, makes an interjection which he pretends is on the same point, but is really on a totally different point, which the barrister did not propose to deal with for days and days to come. When I say "interjection" I mean that he delivers extremely slowly a sentence of inconceivable duration, a sentence so long that it seems really as if it would never end. Finally, the presiding old man decides that it is time it did end, so he interrupts rather testily. Then all the old men frankly abandon the pretence that the barrister has got anything to do with it, and they just argue quietly with each other across the vast red spaces. Meanwhile, the poor men in the pen try to stretch their legs, and mutter fiercely at each other. Four or five of them are immensely distinguished KCs, earning thousands and thousands a year, the very first men in their profession. Yet they tamely submit to being confined in a tiny space where there is no room for their papers, or their tomes, let alone their legs, for days and days and sometimes weeks, with the whole of the House of Lords empty in front of them except for the five old men who spend the day badgering them at ease from comfortable sofas.

To argue a case in the House of Lords must be one of the severest strains to which middle-aged men are ever subjected; it requires tremendous qualities of concentration and patience and intellectual quickness (not to speak of the labour of preparing the cases beforehand). At half-past one, when they have endured this for three hours, they dash out to lunch; they are lucky if they get anything to eat before twenty minutes to two, but at two (presumably because the House of Lords is required for legislative purposes when they have done with it) they have to dash back to the pen again, where digestion must be quite impossible, even if you are not required to argue with the old men. No manual labourer in the world would tolerate such conditions for a day. Either he would break out of the pen and put up his feet on the red benches, or, very sensibly, he would insist that the House of Lords, when sitting as a court, must sit in a place which was suitable for a court, if it was only a committee room in the upper purlieus of the House.

I cannot imagine why the barristers do not say that. It is not as if there was any impressive pomp or ceremony connected with this archaic survival; if there were, it might be worth it. But nothing could be less impressive than these old men mumbling desolately in everyday clothes and beards at rows and rows of empty red sofas. I am told that when the Lord Chancellor presides he does wear robes, but the other Lords still wear mufti. That must be a great sight, but not, I should think, extravagantly solemn.

But perhaps that is the real secret of the British Constitution – our capacity to extract solemnity from the incongruous or the merely dull, I once heard the House of Lords deliver judgment – after days and days of argument – in a case of the highest constitutional importance, involving the rights of the Crown, and what remain of the rights of the subject. All England was waiting with real interest for the issue. One by one the old men read out their long opinions, opinions of great profundity and learning and care, opinions of the greatest judges in the land, universally and rightly respected, opinions that will be quoted in every history and textbook, in every constitutional case, for hundreds of years to come. It took nearly a day to read them. While they were being read, the old men who were not reading, the barristers, the odd dozen of "the public," the clerks, everybody – sat or stood in a sort of coma of stupefied boredom, gazing at nothing. No one stirred. Only, very far away, the gentle voice of the old man might have been heard rolling up to the roof, and squeaking about in the corners, and buzzing about like a sleepy bee under the benches – and always with a faint note of querulous amazement, as if the old man could not believe that anyone was listening to what he was saying. And he was right – for nobody was.

We are a marvellous nation.

LITTLE BITS OF LONDON

II

THE BEAR-GARDEN

The authors of the guide books have signally failed to discover the really interesting parts of Law-land. I have looked through several of these books and not one of them refers, for example, to the "Bear-Garden," which is the place where the preliminary skirmishes of litigation are carried out. The Bear-Garden is the name given to it by the legal profession, so I am quite in order in using the title. In fact, if you want to get to it, you have to use that title. The proper title would be something like The Place where Masters in Chambers function at Half-past One: but if you go into the Law Courts and ask one of the attendants where that is, he will say, rather pityingly, "Do you mean the *Bear-Garden?*" And you will know at once that you have lost caste. Caste is a thing you should be very careful of in these days; so the best thing is to ask for the Bear-Garden straightaway. It is in the purlieus of the Law Courts, and very hard to find. It is up a lot of very dingy back staircases and down a lot of very dingy passages. The Law Courts are like all our public buildings. The parts where the public is allowed to go are fairly respectable, if not beautiful, but the purlieus and the basements and the upper floors are scenes of unimaginable dinginess and decay. The Law Courts' purlieus are worse than the Houses of Parliament purlieus; and it seems to me that even more disgraceful things are done in them. It only shows you the dangers of Nationalization.

On the way to the Bear-Garden you pass the King's Remembrancer's rooms; this is the man who reminds His Majesty about people's birthdays; and in a large family like that he must be kept busy. Not far from the King's Remembrancer there is a Commissioner for Oaths; you can go into his room and have a really good swear for about half a crown. This is cheaper than having it in the street – that is, if you are a gentleman; for by the Profane Oaths Act, 1745, swearing and cursing is punishable by a fine of 1s. for every day-labourer, soldier or seaman; 2s. for every other person under the degree of gentleman; and 5s. for every person of and above the degree of gentleman. This is not generally known. The Commissioner for Oaths is a very broad-minded man, and there is literally no limit to what you may swear before him. The only thing is that he insists on your filing it before you actually say it. This may cause delay, so that if you are feeling particularly strongly about anything, it is probably better to have it out in the street and risk being taken for a gentleman.

There are a number of other interesting functionaries on the way to the Bear-Garden; but we must get on. When you have wandered about in the purlieus for a long time you will hear a

"A really good swear for about half a crown."

tremendous noise, a sort of combined snarling and roaring and legal conversation. When you hear that you will know that you are very near the bears. They are all snarling and roaring in a large preliminary arena, where the bears prepare themselves for the struggle; all round it are smaller cages or arenae, where the struggles take place. If possible, you ought to go early so that you can watch the animals massing. Lawyers, as I have had occasion to observe before, are the most long-suffering profession in the country, and the things they do in the Bear-Garden they have to do in the luncheon hour, or rather in the luncheon half-hour, 1.30 to 2. This accounts, perhaps, for the extreme frenzy of the proceedings. They hurry in in a frenzy up the back stairs about 1.25, and they pace up and down in a frenzy till the time comes. There are all sorts of bears, most of them rather seedy old bears, with shaggy and unkempt coats. These are solicitors' clerks, and they all come straight out of Dickens. They have shiny little private-school handbags, each inherited, no doubt, through a long line of ancestral solicitors' clerks; and they all have the draggled sort of moustache that tells you when it is going to rain. While they are pacing up and down the arena they all try to get rid of these moustaches by pulling violently at alternate ends; but the only result is to make it look more like rain than ever. Some of the bears are robust old bears, with well-kept coats and loud roars; these are solicitors' clerks too, only better-fed; or else they are real solicitors. And a few of the bears are perky young creatures – in barrister's robes – either for the first time – when they look very self-conscious – or for the second time – when they look very self-confident. All the bears are telling each other about their cases. They are saying, "We are a deceased wife's sister suing *in forma pauperis*," or, "I am a discharged bankrupt, three times convicted of perjury, but I am claiming damages under the Diseases of Pigs Act, 1862," or, "You are the crew of a merchant ship and we are the editor of a newspaper – " Just at first it is rather disturbing to hear snatches of conversation like that, but there is no real cause for alarm; they are only identifying themselves with the interests of their clients, and when one realizes that one is a little touched.

At long last one of the keepers at the entrance to the small cages begins to shout very loudly. It is not at all clear what he is shouting, but apparently it is the pet names of the bears, for there is a wild rush for the various cages. Attaching himself to this rush the observer is swept with a struggling mass of bears past the keeper into a cage. Across the middle of the cage a stout barricade has been erected, and behind the barricade sits the Master, pale but defiant. Masters in Chambers are barristers who have not the proper legal faces and have had to give up being ordinary barristers on that account; in the obscurity and excitement of the Bear-Garden nobody notices that their faces are all wrong. The two chief bears rush at the Master and the other bears jostle round them, egging them on. When they see that they cannot get at the Master they begin snarling. One of them snarls quietly out of a long document about the

Statement of Claim. He throws a copy of this at the Master, and the Master tries to get the hang of it while the bear is snarling; but the other bear is by now beside himself with rage and he begins putting in what are called interlocutory snarls, so that the Master gets terribly confused, though he doesn't let on. By and by all pretence of formality and order is put aside, and the battle really begins. At this stage of the proceedings the rule is that not less than two of the protagonists must be roaring at the same time, of which one must be the Master. But the more general practice is for all three of them to roar at the same time. Sometimes, it is true, by sheer roar-power, the Master succeeds in silencing one of the bears for a moment, but he can never be said to succeed in cowing a bear. If anybody is cowed it is the Master. Meanwhile, the lesser bears press closer and closer, pulling at the damp ends of their rainy moustaches and making whispered suggestions for new devilries in the ears of the chief bears, who nod their heads emphatically, but don't pay any attention. The final stage is the stage of physical violence, when the chief bears lean over the barricade and shake their paws at the Master; they think they are only making legal gestures, but the Master knows very well that they are getting out of hand; he knows then that it is time he threw them a bun. So he says a soothing word to each of them and runs his pen savagely through almost everything on their papers. The bears growl in stupefaction and rage, and take deep breaths to begin again. But meanwhile the keeper has shouted for a fresh set of bears, who surge wildly into the room. The old bears are swept aside and creep out, grunting. What the result of it all is I don't know. Nobody knows. The new bears begin snarling...

LITTLE BITS OF LONDON

III

BILLINGSGATE

In order to see Billingsgate properly in action it is necessary to get up at half-past four and travel on the Underground by the first train East, which is an adventure in itself. The first train East goes at three minutes past five, and there are large numbers of people who travel in it every day; by Charing Cross it is almost crowded. It is full of Bolshevists; and I do not wonder. One sits with one's feet up in a first-class carriage, clutching a nice cheap workman's ticket and trying hard to look as if, like the Bolshevists, one did this every day.

On arriving at the Monument Station one walks briskly past the seductive announcement that "The Monument is Now Open," and plunges into a world of fish. I have never been able to understand why fish are so funny. On the comic stage a casual reference to fish is almost certain to provoke a shout of laughter; in practice, and especially in the mass, it is not so funny; it is like the Government, an inexhaustible source of humour at a distance, and in the flesh extraordinarily dull.

Over the small streets which surround the market hangs a heavy pall of fishy vapour. The streets are full of carts; the carts are full of fish. The houses in the streets are fish-dealers' places, more or less full of fish. The pavements are full of fish porters, carrying fish, smelling of fish. Fragments of conversation are heard, all about fish. Fish lie sadly in the gutters. The scales of fish glitter on the pavements. A little vigorous swimming through the outlying fisheries brings you to the actual market, which is even more wonderful. Imagine, a place like Covent Garden, and nearly as big, but entirely devoted to fish. In the place of those enchanting perspectives of flower stalls, imagine enormous regiments of fish stalls, paraded in close order and groaning with halibut and conger eel, with whiting and lobsters and huge crabs. Round these stalls the wholesale dealers wade ankle-deep in fish. Steadily, maliciously, the great fish slide off the stalls on to the floor; steadily the dealers recover them and pile them up on their small counters, or cast them through the air on to other counters, or fling them into baskets in rage or mortification or sheer bravado.

The dealers are men with business-faces, in long white coats, surprisingly clean. Every now and then they stop throwing crabs into baskets or retrieving halibut from the floor, and make little entries in long notebooks. I do not know exactly what entries they make, but I think they must all be in for some competition, and are making notes about their scores; one man I watched had obviously just beaten the record for halibut retrieving. He retrieved so many in about a minute that the tops of his boots were just beginning to show. When he had done that he made such long notes in his book about it that most of the halibut slid on to the floor again while he was doing it. Then he began all over again. But I expect he won the prize.

Meanwhile about a million fish porters are dashing up and down the narrow avenues between the fish stalls, porting millions of boxes of fish. Nearly all of them, I am glad to say, have been in the army or have had a relative in the army; for they are nearly all wearing the full uniform of a company cook, which needs no description. On their heads they have a kind of india-rubber hat, and on the india-rubber hat they have a large box of fish weighing about six stone – six *stone*, I tell you. This box they handle as if it was a box of cigars. They pick it up with a careless gesture; they carry it as if it was a slightly uncomfortable hat, and they throw it down with another careless gesture, usually on to another box of fish; this explains why so many of one's herrings appear to have been maimed at sea.

When they have finished throwing the boxes about they too take out a notebook and make notes about it all. This, it seems, is to make sure that they are paid something for throwing each box about. I don't blame them. It must be a hard life. Yet if I thought I could pick up six stone of salmon and plaice and throw it about I should sign on at Billingsgate at once. It is true they start work about five; but they stop work, it seems, about ten, and they earn a pound and over for that. Then they can go home. Most of them, I imagine, are stockbrokers during the rest of the day.

And they are a refined and gentlemanly body of men. I hope the old legend that the fish porter of Billingsgate expresses himself in terms too forcible for the ordinary man is now exploded; for it is a slander. In fact, it is a slander to call him a "porter"; at least in these days I suppose it is libellous to connect a man falsely with the NUR, if only by verbal implication. But, however that may be, I here assert that the Billingsgate fish

106

porter is a comparatively smooth and courteous personage, and, considering his constant association with fish in bulk, I think it is wonderful.

At the far end of the market is the river Thames; and on the river Thames there is a ship or two, chockful of fish. Fish porters with a kind of *blasé* animation run up and down a long gangway to the ship with six-stone boxes of fine fresh whiting on their heads. These boxes they pile up on a chute (carefully noting each box in their notebooks), after which an auctioneer auctions the boxes. This is the really exciting part of the show. The dealers or the dealers' agents stand round in a hungry ring and buy the boxes of fish as they slide down the chute. The dealers seem to detail a less cultured type of man for this

purpose, and few of the bidders come up to the standard of refinement of the fish porters. But the auctioneer understands them, and he knows all their Christian names. He can tell at a glance whether it is Mossy Isaacs or Sam Isaacs. He is a very clever man.

They stand round looking at the boxes of fish, and when one of them twitches the flesh of his nose or faintly moves one of his eyelashes it means that he has bought six stone of whiting for thirty shillings. That is the only kind of sign they give, and the visitor will be wise not to catch the auctioneer's eye, or blow his nose or do any overt action like that, or he may find that he has bought six stone of salmon and halibut for forty-five shillings. At an auction of fish it is true to say that a nod is as good as a wink; in fact, it is worse.

The dealers are silent, motionless men; but nobody else is. Everybody else is dashing about and shouting as loud as he can. As each box of fish is sold the porters dash at it and shout at it (of course in a very gentlemanly way) and carry it off in all directions. It is quite clear that nobody knows who has bought it or where it is going. The idea of the whole thing is to impress the visitor with the mobility of fish, and this object is successfully attained. No doubt when the visitors have gone away they settle down and decide definitely who is to have the fish.

It is now about half-past six. Fish is still rushing in at one end from the ship and is rushing in at the other from the railway-vans. The porters are throwing the fish at the dealers' stalls (registering each hit in their notebooks), and the dealers are throwing it on to the floor or throwing it at each other or trying to throw it at a retailer, who always puts on a haughty air and passes on to the next stall, till he too gets entangled in the game and finds that he has bought twenty-four stone of whiting at twopence a pound; then he throws it at some more porters, and the porters dash outside and throw it at the carts, and the carts clatter away to Kensington, and my wife buys a whiting at tenpence a pound, and the circle of fish organization is complete.

At about this point it is a good thing to pass on to Covent Garden and buy some flowers.

LITTLE BITS OF LONDON

IV

THE BLOATER SHOW

The last time I was at Olympia – as everybody says at the door – it was a Horse Show. But this time it is much the same. There they stand in their stalls, the dear, magnificent, patient creatures, with their glossy coats and their beautiful curves, their sensitive radiators sniffing for something over the velvet ropes. Panting, I know they are, to be out in the open again; and yet I fancy they enjoy it all in a way. It would be ungrateful if they did not; for, after all, the whole thing has been arranged for them. The whole idea of the Show is to let the motors inspect the bloaters – and not what you think. (You don't know what bloaters are? Well, I can't explain without being rude.)

All the year round they can study *ad nauseam* their own individual bloaters; but this is the only occasion on which they have the whole world of bloaters paraded in front of them for inspection. Now only can they compare notes and exchange grievances.

And how closely they study the parade! Here is a pretty limousine, a blonde; see how she watches the two huge exhibits in front of her. They are very new bloaters, and one of them – oh, horror! – one of them is going to buy. He has never bought before; she knows his sort. He will drive her to death; he may even drive her himself; he will stroke her lovely coat in a familiar, proprietary fashion; he will show her off unceasingly to other bloaters till she is hot all over and the water boils in her radiator. He will hold forth with a horrible intimacy and a yet more horrible ignorance on the most private secrets of her inner life. Not one throb of her young cylinders will be sacred, yet never will he understand her as she would like to be understood. He will mess her with his muddy boots; he will scratch her paint; he will drop tobacco ash all over her cushions – though not from pipes; cigars only…

There – he has bought her. It is a tragedy. Let us move on.

Here is a little *coupé* – a smart young creature with a nice blue coat, fond of town, I should say, but quite at home in the country. She also is inspecting two bloaters. But these two are very shy. In fact, they are not really bloaters at all; they are rather a pair of nice-mannered fresh herrings, not long mated. The male had something to do with that war, I should think; the *coupé* would help him a good deal. The lady likes her because she is dark blue. The other one likes her because of something to do with her works; but he is very reverent and tactful about it. He seems to know that he is being scrutinized, for he is nervous, and scarcely dares to speak about her to the groom in the top hat. He will drive her himself; he will look after her himself; he will know all about her, all about her moods and fancies and secret failings; he will humour and coax her, and she will serve him very nobly.

Already, you see, they have given her a name – "Jane," I think they said; they will creep off into the country with her when the summer comes, all by themselves; they will plunge into the middle of thick forests and sit down happily in the shade at midday and look at her; and she will love them.

But the question is – Ah, they are shaking their heads; they are edging away. She is too much. They look back sadly as they go. Another tragedy…

"Now I am going to be a bloater myself."

Now I am going to be a bloater myself. Here is a jolly one, though her stable-name is much too long. She is a Saloon-de-Luxe and she only costs £2125 (why 5, I wonder – why not 6?). I can run to that, *surely*. At any rate I can climb up and sit down on her cushions; none of the grooms are looking. Dark blue, I see, like Jane. That is the sort of car I prefer. I am like the lady herring; I don't approve of all this talk about the *insides* of things; it seems to me to be rather indecent – unless, of course, you do it very nicely, like that young herring. When you go and look at a horse you don't ask how its sweetbread is arranged, or what is the principle of its liver. Then why should you…?

Well, here we are, and very comfortable too. But why do none of these cars have any means of communication between the owner and the man next to the chauffeur? There is always a telephone to the chauffeur, but none to the overflow guest on the box. So that when the host sees an old manor house which he thinks the guest hasn't noticed he has to hammer on the glass and do semaphore; and the guest thinks he is being asked if he is warm enough.

Otherwise, though, this is a nice car. It is very cosy in here. Dark, and quiet, and warm. I could go to sleep in here.

What? What's that? No, I don't really want to buy it, thank you. I just wanted to see if it was a good sleeping car. As a matter of fact I think it is. But I don't like the colour. And what I really want is a *cabriolet*. Good afternoon. Thank you…

A pleasant gentleman, that. I wish I could have bought the saloon. She would have liked me. So would he, I expect.

Well, we had better go home. I shan't buy any more cars today. And we won't go up to the gallery; there is nothing but oleo plugs and graphite grease up there. That sort of thing spoils the romance.

Ah, here is dear Jane again! What a pity it was – Hullo, they have come back – that nice young couple. They are bargaining – they are beating him down. No, he is beating them up. Go on

– go on. Yes, you can run to that – *of course* you can. Sell those oil shares. Look at her – *look* at her! You can't leave her here for one of the bloaters. He wavers; he consults. "Such a lovely colour." Ah, that's done it! He has decided. He has bought. She has bought. They have bought. Hurrah!

LITTLE BITS OF LONDON

V

BOND STREET

I find it very difficult to walk slowly down Bond Street as one ought to do; I always feel so guilty. Most of the people there look scornfully at me as if I belonged to Whitechapel, and the rest look suspiciously at me as if I belonged to Bond Street. My clothes are neither good enough nor bad enough. So I hurry through with the tense expression of a man who is merely using Bond Street as a thoroughfare, because it is the way to his dentist – as indeed in my case it is. But recently I *did* saunter in the proper way, and I took a most thrilling inventory of the principal classes of shops, the results of which have now been tabulated by my statistical department.

For instance, do you know how many shops in the street sell things for ladies to wear (not including boots, jewellery or shoes)? No? Well, there are thirty-three. Not many, is it? But then there are twenty-one jewellers (including pearl shops) and eight boot and/or shoe shops; so that, with two sort of linen places, which may fairly be reckoned as female, the ladies' total is sixty-four. I only counted a hundred and fifty shops altogether. Of that total, nine are places where men can buy things to wear, and ten are places where they can buy things to smoke; I have charitably debited all the cigarette shops to the

"I feel so guilty."

men, even the ones where the cigarettes are tipped with rose leaves and violet petals. But even if I do that and give the men the two places where you can buy guns and throw in the one garden-seat shop, we are left with the following result:

FEMININE SHOPS		MASCULINE SHOPS.	
Dress	33	Dress	9
Jewellers	21	Tobacco	10
Boots and Shoes	8	Motors	9
Sort of Linen Places	2	Guns	2
Dog Bureau	1	Garden Seats	1
	65		31

From these figures a firm of Manchester actuaries has drawn the startling conclusion that Bond Street is more used by women than by men. It may be so. But a more interesting question is, how do all these duplicates manage to carry on, considering the very reasonable prices they charge? At one point there are three jewellers in a row, with another one opposite. Not far off there are three cigarette shops together, madly defying each other with gold tips and silver tips, cork tips and velvet tips, rose tips and lily tips. There is only one bookshop, of course, but there are about nine picture-places. How do they all exist? It is mysterious.

Especially when you consider how much trouble they take to avoid attracting attention. There are still one or two window-dressers who lower the whole tone of the street by adhering to the gaudy-overcrowded style; but the majority, in a violent reaction from that, seem to have rushed to the wildest extremes of the simple-unobtrusive. They are delightful, I think, those reverent little windows with the chaste curtains and floors of polished walnut, in the middle of which reposes delicately a single toque, a single chocolate, or a single pearl. Some of the picture-places are among the most modest. There is one window which suggests nothing but the obscure branch of a highly decayed bank in the dimmest cathedral town. On the dingy screen which entirely fills the window is written simply in letters which time has almost erased, "JOHN SMITH – Pictures." Nothing could be less enticing. Yet inside, I daresay, fortunes are made daily. I noticed no trace of this method at the Advertisers' Exhibition; they might give it a trial.

Now no doubt you fondly think that Bond Street is wholly devoted to luxuries; perhaps you have abandoned your dream of actually buying something in Bond Street? You are wrong. To begin with, there are about ten places where you can buy food, and, though there is no pub now, there is a café (with a licence). There are two grocers and a poulterer. There is even a fish shop – you didn't know that, did you? I am bound to say it seemed to have only the very largest fish, but they were obviously fish.

Anyone can go shopping in Bond Street. I knew a clergyman once who went in and asked for a back-stud. He was afterwards unfrocked for riotous living, but the stud was produced. You can buy a cauliflower in Bond Street – if you know the ropes. There is a shop which merely looks like a very beautiful florist's. There are potatoes in the window, it is true, but they are "hot-house" ones; inside there is no trace of a common vegetable. But if you ask facetiously for a cauliflower (as I did) the young lady will disappear below ground and actually return with a real cauliflower (*de luxe*, of course). I remember few more embarrassing episodes.

And if you like to inquire at the magnificent provision-merchant's he too will conjure up from the magic cellars boot cream and metal polish and all those vulgar groceries which make life possible. That is the secret of Bond Street. Beneath that glittering display of luxurious trivialities there are vast reserves of solid prosaic necessaries, only waiting to be asked for. A man could live exclusively on Bond Street. I don't know where you would buy your butchers' meat, but I have a proud fancy that, if you went in and said something to one of those sleek and sorrowful jewellers, he too would vanish underground and blandly return to you with a jewelled steak or a plush chop.

"A plush chop."

Many years ago, they tell me, there *was* a butcher in Bond Street. Perhaps you dealt there. For my part I was not eating much meat in those days. But I can imagine his window – a perfect little grotto of jasper and onyx, with stalactites of pure gold, and in the middle, resting on a genuine block of Arctic ice, an exquisite beef sausage. I wish he would come back.

It is difficult to realize that there is anything but shop windows in Bond Street, but I like to think that, up there in those upper stories which one never sees, there does dwell a self-contained little community for whom Bond Street is merely the village street, down which the housewives pass gossiping each morning to the greengrocer's or the fishmonger's, and never purchase any pearls at all.

When the butcher comes back I think I shall join them.

THE LITTLE GUIGGOLS

[I understand that there is a dearth of the kind of horrible little plays which the public really wants. It ought not to be difficult to meet that want. Nearly everybody I know is good at dialogue but can't do plots; personally I teem with plots, but am not so good at dialogue. So I propose to present you with the ground plan – the *scenario* – of a few really sensational, thrilling and, on the whole, unpleasant playlets, and you can do the rest.)

I

THE MISSING STAR
(*Based on an old legend, and also, I am sorry to say, on fact.*)

The scene is the interior of a small tent at a country fair. Through the open door can be seen the back of Bert, who is shouting madly, "Walk up! Walk up! Now showin' – the Performin' Fleas! Edward! Edward! Does everything but talk. Walk up! Walk up!" Seven or eight people file sheepishly into the tent and stand reverently in front of the small table under the single bright light – a soldier and his love, two small boys, a highly respectable mater and paterfamilias, with Reginald in an Eton collar, also a young man who may be a barrister, or possibly one of those writing fellows. They do not look at each other; *they are ashamed.*

The red velvet curtain is drawn across the door of the tent, muffling the wild noises of the fair.

Mr Slint, the little showman, adjusts his gold pince-nez and speaks; the audience close round the table and crane their necks. Mr Slint speaks in the patronizing, almost contemptuous, tones of the expert lecturer who has something unique to offer.

Mr Slint (quietly). I now show you the Performing Fleas. The fleas are common fleas, trained by myself. Perseverance and patience is alone required.

The Writing Fellow (intelligently). You never use the whip?

Mr Slint (taking no notice). Now the nature of the flea is to 'op; it is *not* the nature of the flea to walk. I 'ave trained the fleas to walk. I will now show you the flea as newly captured. Being still untrained, 'e still 'ops, you see.

He produces a miniature kennel, to which is attached "by a 'uman 'air" an undeniable flea. The flea hops gallantly, but is clearly impeded from doing its best jumps by the human hair.

We are now shown a second flea which is "only half-trained." He has certainly forgotten how to hop. Indeed he seems to be suffering from congenital inertia. He scrambles a centimetre or two and sometimes makes a sort of flutter off the ground, but he rather suggests a solicitor learning to fly than a flea learning to walk.

Mr S. I will now show you the flea when fully trained.

He opens a small cardboard box which seems to be full of toy four-wheelers and hansom cabs. They are made of some metal, brightly painted, with substantial metal wheels. One of these vehicles is placed on the lighted board and begins to move. It is drawn by Eustace. It moves at a steady pace towards the materfamilias.

Reginald (suddenly, in a high piping voice). How does he feed them, mother?

The Materfamilias. Hush, dear.

Mr S (impassive). The fleas are fed on the 'uman arm. (*An afterthought*) My own.

Reginald (an imaginative child). Does he feed them one at a time, or all together, mother?

"The Missing Star."

The MF. Hush, dear.

Mr S. I will now show you Edward, champion flea of the world.

Edward is indeed a magnificent creature. He is drawing a light racing hansom and he shows an amazing turn of speed. Eustace with his heavy old four-wheeler has a long start, but in a moment Edward is up with him; he has passed him.

Reginald (breathlessly). Mother, he's *running*!

And so he is. He is making a beeline for the MF. *Will he reach her?* No. Mr Slint has coolly picked up Edward's hansom and is showing him to the spectators through a magnifying glass. The limelight is thrown on to Edward's swarthy features and by an ingenious use of the cinema we are now shown a striking "close up" of Edward's expression as he is passed round before the people in the tent, hanging in his tiny collar at the end of the human hair. Rage, hatred, mortification, boredom, and what can only be described as the lust for blood are indicated in turn by the rolling eyes, the mobile lips. And, as he passes before the MF, he wears a look of thwarted ambition which makes one shudder.

Now comes the final spectacle. Out of the little box Mr Slint rapidly takes cab after cab and sets them on the white board, line abreast. Each cab is drawn by a single devoted flea. On the right of the line is Edward, on the left is Eustace. In perfect order the fleas advance, dressing by the right...

It is a moving sight. There is something very sinister in that steady, noiseless, calculated progress – for I need not say that the fleas are moving *away* from Mr Slint: they are moving with machine-like precision towards Reginald. No, they have changed direction. Edward has given them "Right incline!" They are moving with machine-like precision, silent, inexorable, cabs and all, towards the materfamilias.

R (shrilly, still worried). Do they have to be unharnessed for meals, mother?

The MF. Hush, dear.

Mr Slint purrs on about his patience and perseverance. Suddenly there is a stir on the right of the line; there has been an accident; Edward's wheels are locked with the careless four-wheeler's on his left. A scurry, a sharp cry from Mr Slint and Edward has disappeared.

Mr Slint acts promptly. The door of the tent is barred. He announces to the cowering spectators that a valuable artiste is missing and that those present are to be searched before leaving. (*He suspects foul play.*)

Suddenly he makes a dart at the MF and from her shoulder – oh, horror! – he takes a *Thing*. "Larceny!" he cries; "I mean abduction. Quick, Bert, the police."

The Paterfamilias. Spare her, sir. She is a mother.

A policeman (*entering*). Now then, what's this 'ere?

Mr S (*moved by who knows what chivalrous impulse*). Madam, I have wronged you. This is not Edward. It is one of yours. (*He replaces the Thing.*)

The MF (*shrieking*). Oh, oh! The *shame* of it!

Reginald. I know, mother! Put it on the table. If it's Edward it will walk: if it's one of – if it's not, it will hop.

The Thing is placed solemnly upon the table. All crowd round and watch for the issue. The flea does not walk. On the other hand it does not hop. Nothing happens. The flea is dead.

So no one will ever know.

The MF swoons away…

CURTAIN

THE LITTLE GUIGGOLS

II
THE LURCH

[*Tyltyl*. It seems hardly worth while, then, to take so much
trouble. – *The Betrothal*.]

I am afraid this little Guiggol has somehow got mixed up with
M. Maeterlinck; but the two schools have, of course, a good deal
in common, so it should work out fairly well.

The play opens in The Place Which is Neither Here nor
There; it seems to be a high hill entirely surrounded by fog. The
unfortunate *Bill Tyl* and his sister *Methyl** are doing their utmost
to die, driven on by the sinister figure of *Indigestion*, which
grows larger and larger as the play progresses. They meet with a
good deal of opposition in their simple project, and when the
play begins they have already been to The House of Uncles and
The Abode of the Half-Baked for permission to die; but they
always find that before they can do it they have to go to just *one*
more place for information and advice. It is like walking up one
of those tiresome mountains which never seem to have a top;
or it is like trying to find out which Government Department is
really responsible; or it is like... But enough.

Bill and *Methyl* have now been told that they cannot die until
they have gone down and rescued all the people who have been

*Who afterwards gave her name to the celebrated spirits.

125

left in The Lurch during their lives; so they are discovered standing on the hill preparing to go down into The Lurch. *Indigestion* endeavours to dissuade them, saying that they had much better go down the other side of the hill into The Limbo. But the seductive figure of *Food* intervenes, gorgeously dressed in aspic, and eventually prevails.

At this point there is a jolly bit of dialogue:

Bill (*profoundly*). Food is good.

The Oldest Uncle (*I forget how he got there*). Food is very good.

Food (*mysteriously*). The food which you eat is good, but the food which you do not eat is better.

Methyl (*frightened*). What does she mean?

Bill. I do not know what she means.

Food. I do not know what I mean.

The OU. I do not know what the author means.

M. Does anybody know what he means?

Indigestion. He does not mean anything.

Bill. Oh, oh! I wish he would mean something.

Ind. He is pulling your leg.

The next scene is The Lurch itself, a very horrible place, where we see all the people who have been left in it wishing they could get out of it; at least we don't see them because the whole place is full of a dense fog; but they are there, groping about and contemplating unutterably the opaque immensities of boredom. Their hands move invisibly through the vast gloom, plying the instruments of Destiny; most of them are knitting. You see, they are nearly all old maids. None of them can be got out of The Lurch until those who left them in it remember them and return. There are also, of course, large crowds of old men in all stages of decay. Many of them are Colonels who have been left in The Lurch by the Government, and naturally there is no hope for them. It is all extremely sad.

In low tones they do a little dialogue, like sheep bleating on the Mountains of Eternity.

The Oldest Old Maid. Will he never come?

"The Lurch."

The Oldest Old Maid But One. He will never come.

A Frightfully Old Man. The fog is very foggy.

The OOM. It is difficult to see things in a fog.

The OOMBO. If he came I should not see him.

An Awfully Old Colonel. You are lucky.

The OOMBO. I am not lucky.

The OOM. She is not lucky.

A FOM. There must be some mistake.

An AOC. You are not waiting for the Government. That is what I meant.

The OOM. Oh, oh! He meant something.

A FOM. There must be some mistake.

The OOMBO. Oh, oh! Somebody is coming.

Bill and his party come in on all fours. You cannot see them because of the fog, but you can hear them coughing. It is terrible. There is a scene of intense intensity while *Bill Tyl* and *Methyl* crawl about trying to find the people they have come to find. *Bill* keeps finding the *Awfully Old Colonel* by mistake, and this causes a great deal of emotion. The one he is after is *The Oldest Old Maid But One*, and, as she says nothing but "Oh, Oh, I cannot smell him," instead of saying, "Here I am, Bill," it is very difficult to identify her.

But suddenly *Methyl* remembers that in all her blameless life *she has never left anyone in The Lurch*. (Woodwind, *sotto voce* – and strings, *vibrato*.) The rule is that anyone who comes down to The Lurch and remembers things like that may rescue everyone who is in The Lurch at the time.

This gives general satisfaction and the whole party sets off to the top, Old Maids and all.

In the next scene we are back at The Place Which Is Neither Here Nor There again, only now we have a splendid view of The Place of Ecstasy and The Golden Sea. Also a little to the left we see the yawning chasms of The Limbo (which is only one better than The Lurch).

The Place of Ecstasy is top-hole. Gleaming unspeakably in the unimaginable radiance of the inconceivable light (80 watts), immense columns of barley sugar melt away into space, avenue by avenue, while just below in The Golden Sea, which is entirely composed of the finest golden syrup, wallow in a refined manner Those Who Have Arrived.

The travellers feast their eyes on this vision of bliss. And now comes the terrible, Guiggolian thrill. There has been a good deal of dialogue on the way up from The Lurch, and poor Bill has been brooding gloomily over the prospect of spending eternity in the same company.

All the *Old Birds* are standing in a violet haze of ineffable gladness on the brink, with joyous springs of orangeade bubbling at their feet and castor sugar descending in showers all round, when Bill has a very naughty impulse, which I regret to say he makes no attempt to resist.

He pushes the whole crowd of *Old Birds* over into The Limbo. Then with a great cry of joy he and *Methyl* plunge into the Golden Sea...

Food and *Indigestion* are left behind – immutable, eternal...

CURTAIN

THE LITTLE GUIGGOLS

III

NUMBER SEVEN
(*Based on an old legend*)

A Room in the East. Some time ago. A Man and a Woman having supper.

She. You eat heartily, my pomegranate.

He. Yes, I am hungry. And I am happy, for is it not our bridal feast?

She. That reminds me. There is something I want to tell you. As a matter of fact I meant to tell you before, but I have been so busy buying clothes.

He. Oh, what is that? Pass the salt.

She (passing). The fact is, you are not my first husband; at least, not exactly.

He. How do you mean?

She. As a matter of fact you are the – the first but five.

He (working it out). I see. I take it the others are away from home.

She (gently). No. They died. Have some more salad?

He. Thank you. I'm sorry. At least, you know what I mean.

She. The odd thing was that they all died at the same time – in a way.

He. Oh! Was there an epidemic, or what?

She. Oh, no. What I mean is they each died the night we were married.

He. That *is* curious. Why did they die?

She. Nobody knows. They just died. It's given me a great deal of bother.

He. But I suppose you've been able to use the same trousseau in each case?

She. But nay; for I have invariably embroidered every garment in gold and silver with the name and image of my love.

He. By Jove, what a bore! I say, have you embroidered any garments with *my* name and image? I'd like to see them.

She (*sadly*). Nay, my beloved. This time I have embroidered nothing. It seemed such a waste.

He. Yes, yes, of course. All the same – You know, my olive branch, I can't help wishing you'd told me about this before we were wed.

She. I am sorry, my love. I can't think how it slipped my memory. But there was so much shopping to be done, and what with one thing and another – *Do* have some more salad.

He. Thanks; it's delicious. By the way, who made it?

She. With her own fair hands your lily contrived it.

He. Oh! Perhaps, after all, I won't have any more. I don't feel so hungry as I thought I did.

She. The last but two used to love my salads. All his married life –

He (*musing*). By the way, when you say "night," what time of night do you mean? When did the last but two, for instance –

She. I should have said "evening" really; it was careless of me. Usually about nine –

He (*looking at hour glass*). Curious – I don't feel nearly so well. I wonder if –

[*The Curtain falls to denote the passage of a few months. When it rises two people are discovered at supper – a Woman (the same one) and a Man (a different one).*

She. You eat heartily, my pomegranate.

He. Who would not eat heartily on the day of his espousal to such a maid as *thee*?

She. That reminds me. I knew there was something I wanted to tell you, but the wedding put it quite out of my head.

He. Truly, what shouldest thou think of at thy espousal but thy spouse?

She. Do you mind saying "*you*"? None of the others have said "*thou*."

He. As you will, beloved. But of what "others" speakest thou?

She. Well, that's really the point. The fact is, my tangerine, you are not my first spouse – at least, not quite.

He. How so? What delicious salad!

She. Have some more. No, you are – let me see – one, two, three, four – yes, you are the first but six. It's rather a curious story; I wonder if it would bore you?

He. What tale from thy sweet lips could tedious be?

She. I wish you'd get out of that "*thy*" habit; it's so irritating. Well, the fact is that all your predecessors died on the evening of our wedding – I mean weddings – and nobody quite knows why.

He. Truly a strange tale. May I have just *one* more go at the salad?

She. Of course. I'm so glad you like it. Curiously enough, the one before you was very fond of it too; in fact I've often wondered – Well, there it is. Now I do hope that nothing is going to happen to you, my dear, because I should so hate to think that you had been put to any inconvenience on my account. Besides, it upsets the servants.

He. Have no fear, beloved. For I too have a secret. I *know* thy – your – tragic history; a witch has revealed it unto me.

She. You *know*? Well, I do think you might have told me. I meant it to be a surprise.

He. Further, she has given me a magic charm to protect us both.

"Number Seven."

She. I say, what's that mess in the corner? There – on the plate.

He. That is the heart and liver of a fish, my apple.

She. I hope you haven't brought a cat into the house; father can't bear them.

He. Nay, my love, that is the charm.

She. It looks a very large one. What fish is it?

He. It is the heart and liver of a sturgeon.

She. I suppose it couldn't have been done with an anchovy?

He. Nay, nay. For the witch enjoined me; first I must burn it –

She. Yes, I think you'd better.

He. See? (*burns*). The ashes thereof will drive away the evil spirit that molests you.

She (*recoiling*). And I don't wonder.

[*The Curtain falls, and rises again the next morning. The room is full of smoke.*

He (*shaving*). Who is that man digging in the garden?

She. Oh, that's father. He's digging a grave for you. It's become a sort of habit with him.

He. Wilt thou not tell him it is not required?

She (*through the window*). Father, we shan't want it this time. Sorry.

He. I thank thee.

She (*irritable*). Oh, do stop saying "*thee.*" And will you please take these horrible ashes and throw them away *at once*? Really, I can hardly breathe.

He. Nay, my love. They are our charm against danger. Art not thou – I mean, aren't you grateful?

She. Yes, of course. But they've done the trick by now. We can't spend our whole married life in this atmosphere.

He. But indeed we must. The witch enjoined me that, unless they were preserved, I should perish, even as those before me.

She. Well, I'm extremely sorry, but I really can't stand this. (*Through the window*) Father, you might bury this, will you? (*throws down the ashes*). Thank you. Oh, and don't fill up the hole yet. We may want it after all.

CURTAIN

A P Herbert

A.P.H. His Life and Times

In 1970 the inimitable A P Herbert turned eighty and celebrated becoming the latest octogenarian by publishing his autobiography. Already much admired and loved for his numerous articles, essays, books, plays, poetry and musicals and his satirical outlook on the world, this time he turns his gaze to his own life and examines the events that brought him to his eightieth birthday – Winchester and Oxford, Gallipoli and France, and then, in 1924, to the staff of *Punch* where he remained for sixty years delighting readers with his regular column.

Alan Herbert was very much an Englishman and a gentleman – outspoken patriot, defender of the good and denouncer of injustice – and, in everything, he retained his sense of fun. And this zest for life that saw him through so much will delight readers as they delve into the life of this great man.

Honeybubble & Co.

Mr Honeybubble proved to be one of A P Herbert's most popular creations and avid readers followed his progress through life in A P H's column in *Punch* where he first appeared. Here his exploits are collected together with a cast of other colourful characters from the riches of their creator's imagination. *Honeybubble & Co.* is a delightful series of sketches revealing some of the more humorous aspects of the human nature.

A P Herbert

Number Nine

Admiral of the Fleet the Earl of Caraway and Stoke is, as one might expect being an Admiral, a man of the sea. In fact, so much so that for him, all the world's a ship, and all the men and women merely sailors…

The Admiral's dedication to King and country could never be questioned – but surely it was a bit much expecting him to give up his ancestral home for the psychological testing of candidates for the Civil Service. Tired of the constant intrusion, and aided and abetted by his son Anthony and the lovely Peach, he embarks upon a battle of wits against the political hopefuls. The result is a hilarious tale of double-crossing, eavesdropping – and total mayhem.

The Old Flame

Robin Moon finds Phyllis rather a distraction in the Sunday morning service – after all her golden hair does seem to shine rather more brightly than the Angel Gabriel's heavenly locks. His wife, Angela, on the other hand, is more preoccupied with the cavalier Major Trevor than perhaps she should be during the Litany. Relations between the Moons head towards an unhappy crescendo, and when, after an admirable pot-luck Sunday lunch, Robin descends to the depths of mentioning what happened on their honeymoon, the result is inevitable – they must embark on one of their enforced separations. Finding his independence once more, Robin feels free to link up with Phyllis and her friends, and begins to dabble in some far from innocent matchmaking.

This ingenious work brilliantly addresses that oh so perplexing a problem – that of 'the old flame'.

A P Herbert

The Thames

A P Herbert lived by the Thames for many years and was a fervent campaigner for its preservation and up-keep. Here, in this beautifully descriptive history, he uses his love and knowledge of the mighty river to tell its story from every aspect – from its dangerous currents to its tranquil inlets, and from its cities and bridges to its people and businesses. Adding his renowned wisdom and wit to his vast knowledge, A P Herbert creates a fascinating and entertaining guided tour of the Thames, and offers his own plans for the river's future. This is the perfect companion for lovers of both London and her waterways.

A P Herbert

Topsy, MP

Fresh from 'Earth's *rosiest* honeymoon since Adam and Eve', Topsy returns to a life of marital bliss, and finds herself '*too* unanimously' elected a Member of Parliament. Social functions and parliamentary and wifely duties aside, she somehow still finds time to pour out her thoughts on her new life to the devoted Trix. In this latest collection of letters, she remains as endearing as ever and her deliberations, preoccupations and observations retain their candid freshness – and make hilarious reading.

'my dear you know I'm a *comparative* fundamentalist in dogmatological matters' [Topsy on principles]

'he was so beflattened that the little *feminine* heart was *totally* melted, and besides it's *quite* my policy to conciliate rather than *inflame* the foe' [Topsy on the Opposition]

OTHER TITLES BY A P HERBERT AVAILABLE DIRECT
FROM HOUSE OF STRATUS

Quantity		£	$(US)	$(CAN)	€
	A.P.H. His Life and Times	9.99	16.50	24.95	16.50
	General Cargo	7.99	12.95	19.95	14.50
	Honeybubble & Co.	7.99	12.95	19.95	14.50
	The House by the River	7.99	12.95	19.95	14.50
	Look Back and Laugh	7.99	12.95	19.95	14.50
	Made For Man	7.99	12.95	19.95	14.50
	The Man About Town	7.99	12.95	19.95	14.50
	Mild and Bitter	7.99	12.95	19.95	14.50
	More Uncommon Law	8.99	14.99	22.50	15.00
	Number Nine	7.99	12.95	19.95	14.50
	The Old Flame	7.99	12.95	19.95	14.50
	The Secret Battle	7.99	12.95	19.95	14.50
	Sip! Swallow!	7.99	12.95	19.95	14.50
	The Thames	10.99	17.99	26.95	18.00
	Topsy, MP	7.99	12.95	19.95	14.50
	Topsy Turvy	7.99	12.95	19.95	14.50
	Trials of Topsy	7.99	12.95	19.95	14.50
	Uncommon Law	9.99	16.50	24.95	16.50
	The Water Gipsies	8.99	14.99	22.50	15.00
	What a Word!	7.99	12.95	19.95	14.50

ALL HOUSE OF STRATUS BOOKS ARE AVAILABLE FROM GOOD BOOKSHOPS
OR DIRECT FROM THE PUBLISHER:

Internet: www.houseofstratus.com including synopses and features.

Email: sales@houseofstratus.com please quote author, title and credit card details.

Order Line: UK: 0800 169 1780,
USA: 1 800 509 9942
INTERNATIONAL: +44 (0) 20 7494 6400 (UK)
or +01 212 218 7649
(please quote author, title, and credit card details.)

Send to: House of Stratus Sales Department   House of Stratus Inc.
24c Old Burlington Street   Suite 210
London   1270 Avenue of the Americas
W1X 1RL   New York • NY 10020
UK   USA

PAYMENT

Please tick currency you wish to use:

☐ £ (Sterling)   ☐ $ (US)   ☐ $ (CAN)   ☐ € (Euros)

Allow for shipping costs charged per order plus an amount per book as set out in the tables below:

CURRENCY/DESTINATION

	£(Sterling)	$(US)	$(CAN)	€(Euros)
Cost per order				
UK	1.50	2.25	3.50	2.50
Europe	3.00	4.50	6.75	5.00
North America	3.00	3.50	5.25	5.00
Rest of World	3.00	4.50	6.75	5.00
Additional cost per book				
UK	0.50	0.75	1.15	0.85
Europe	1.00	1.50	2.25	1.70
North America	1.00	1.00	1.50	1.70
Rest of World	1.50	2.25	3.50	3.00

PLEASE SEND CHEQUE OR INTERNATIONAL MONEY ORDER.
payable to: STRATUS HOLDINGS plc or HOUSE OF STRATUS INC. or card payment as indicated

STERLING EXAMPLE

Cost of book(s):..................... Example: 3 x books at £6.99 each: £20.97
Cost of order: .... Example: £1.50 (Delivery to UK address)
Additional cost per book:.............. Example: 3 x £0.50: £1.50
Order total including shipping:.......... Example: £23.97

VISA, MASTERCARD, SWITCH, AMEX:

☐☐☐☐☐☐☐☐☐☐☐☐☐☐☐☐☐☐☐

Issue number (Switch only):

☐☐☐

Start Date: Expiry Date:

☐☐/☐☐   ☐☐/☐☐

Signature: _____

NAME: _____

ADDRESS: _____

COUNTRY: _____

ZIP/POSTCODE: _____

Please allow 28 days for delivery. Despatch normally within 48 hours.

Prices subject to change without notice.
Please tick box if you do not wish to receive any additional information. ☐

House of Stratus publishes many other titles in this genre; please check our website (**www.houseofstratus.com**) for more details.